The Broadale Stone Recipe book

GW00374277

Compiled and Published by
GEERINGS OF ASHFORD LTD.

Illustrations by Barbara Seth

ISBN 1 873953 24 0

Designed and printed by Geerings of Ashford Limited
Cobbs Wood House, Chart Road, Ashford, Kent TN23 1EP

CONTENTS

Brogdale Stone Fruit

Whisper it softly but there are those who don't think too much of stone fruit.

Ask them to name their favourite fruit and you can be sure that the apple, pear or strawberry will top their list. To these poor souls, plums and apricots lack a certain glamour; prunes have a problem with PR.

This collection of Stone Fruit recipes shows exactly what they are missing.

Britain's stone fruit hold a world of opportunity for the cook and a world of flavour for the rest of us to enjoy. They can be eaten as fresh fruit, pies, puddings and desserts. They can be preserved and pickled.

In an age of supermarket shopping, plucking a plum from a fruit-laden branch is a simple pleasure that many have forgotten. So while for some, this volume will be a timely reminder of the value and versatility of our stone fruit. For others it will serve as an introduction.

CHERRIES

Life, it is said, is a bowl of cherries. Each new fruit a fresh experience to be savoured. Some will thrill, others, inevitably, fall a little flat.

The ripe, plump cherry has presented painters and writers with an image of voluptuousness which they have returned to time and time again. Dutch painters of the 17th century captured the perfection of the ripe cherry while generations of poets and songwriters have likened the lush lips of woman to the bursting, sensual fruit.

Despite the cherry's place in literature, art and music, our purpose in here is to provide a somewhat more prosaic introduction.

3

Sweet and sour cherries were cultivated around the mediterranean Before Christ and the fruit takes its name from the Greek Kerasos. By the 1st century AD, cultivation was common in Italy and records show that the cherry was grown in Britain at that time.

However, the Fall of the Roman Empire marked the beginning of the decline of the Cherry in Britain, a decline reversed by its reintroduction in the 17th Century.

While Kent is, without doubt, Britain's major cherry growing region, France and Italy are the prime growers on mainland Europe while California and Washington are the most productive parts of North America. So popular is the fruit that there are now some 900 varieties of sweet cherry and 300 sour varieties.

There are two main groups of sweet cherry; the firm, dry fleshed biggarreau and the softer, juicier guigne varieties. Likewise, the sour varieties fall into two categories: amarelle which are light coloured with clear juice, and griotte which are darker and have coloured juice.

While it is the sweet cherry which is normally eaten in its natural state, sour cherries have ruled the culinary roost. Cherries are used in pies and many other desserts and in some parts of northern Europe, even as a soup. For preserves and baking, the black Morello cherry is the prime choice. The Morello is also the basis for the Cherry liqueur, Kirsch.

PLUMS

Like other members of the Prunus species, the Plum is a member the rose family and is found growing naturally across the world from the Pacific Coast of the USA to Japan.

Closely related to the cherry which it resembles in all but size, Plums are rich in vitamin A and contain a large number of mineral salts. Plums are delicious eaten raw and can be used as a cooked compote with desserts or to accompany meats including lamb and pork. Plums also make excellent jams, preserves, chutneys and pickles.

4

plum is, to the uninitiated something of a mystery. When erence is made to the Plum, most of us think of the Prunus mestica, the garden or European plum, once considered a species s own right but now listed as a hybrid. A number of other fruit, h with its own name, may also lay claim to being a Plum. Indeed, he middle ages, plum was the name used for almost any dried t and used in pies and puddings. When little Jack Horner sat in corner, it may well not have been a plum which emerged when plunged his thumb into his Christmas Pie.

er types of Plum are:

E BULLACE which grows wild in Europe and bears small, nd, usually black fruits.

E DAMSON, a small Plum from the East which demands to be ked with plenty of sugar.

E GREENGAGE. A plum introduced to England by Sir Thomas e around 1725 from France where it is known as Reine Claude. engages are considered the finest of dessert plums and while y consider them best eaten uncooked, they make an excellent n jam.

E MIRABELLE is a French plum, similar to Damsons and ace, thought to have arrived in Europe from the East in the 15th tury.

E CHERRY PLUM or myrobalan is associated with the casus region.

E SLOE or blackthorn grows wild in hedgerows throughout pe and the west of Asia. The small black fruits make excellent and give a particular piquancy to gin.

introduction to plums would be complete without mention of es, the dried plum commonly detested by schoolchildren but ed by others for its flavour and contribution to an effective stive system.

Not all plums make good prunes. They must, for example, have a high sugar content and a relatively small stone.

California produces most of the world's prunes although there are prune industries in Algeria, Iraq, Jordan, Spain and today even Australia.

APRICOTS

Lovers of the apricot owe a debt to the Chinese who first recognised the potential of the fruit and began cultivation before 2000BC.

Arab traders ensured the westward spread of the fruit in Africa and around the Mediterranean before the Romans brought it to Europe. By the 16th century it was popular in the gardens of England's landed classes and, as the Europeans set off to discover new worlds, they took the apricot with them . . . to the USA, South Africa, New Zealand and Australia.

Although the fresh apricot has a particular appeal, most of the harvest is consigned to be processed in one way or another. Apricot jam is not simply a joy in its own right but an important ingredient for bakers who use it as a glaze and as a glue which, among other things, sticks icing to cakes.

The apricot can be preserved in a number of ways. It may be bottled in syrup or brandy, tinned, made into jam or used in pickles and sweetmeats.

The versatility of the apricot is perhaps best demonstrated in the Middle East where it is used in sweetmeats - perhaps stuffed with almonds or almond paste, or to accompany meat.

Many would agree that apricots make the best dried fruits because of their ability to keep their flavour. While most are prepared by modern process which involves bleaching and re-colouring the fruit, the finest dried apricots are produced by natural sun-drying.

PEACHES

The peach enjoys an unusual place in our affections. While it is a long way from being the most exotic of fruit, it has a reputation for being the most erotic due, we are told, to the fact that the ripe peach comes closest of all fruits to resembling human flesh.

Its succulent and downy skin put the peach ahead of even the pear and cherry when it comes to erotic metaphor.

Like the apricot, the peach was a native of China where it still grows wild. However, the wild peaches of China are small and sour and a host of new, improved varieties have been developed during the past 2,000 years or so.

The ancient Persians are thought to have introduced the peach to their country with such success that it came to be regarded as a native Persian fruit. Scholars certainly tell us that the fruit was known in Europe before the first Century BC and, judging by the evidence of frescos and other paintings, the size of peaches enjoyed in Roman times were equal to those we find today. With most other fruit, early cultivars were smaller than their successors.

That the Anglo Saxons had a word - perseoc-treou - for the peach suggests it was introduced into England at an early stage and by the reign of Elizabeth I, many, mostly French, varieties were being cultivated in England.

the 16th Century, the Spanish took the peach with them to Latin America and by the following century it was being grown in California. The spread continued to Australia and South Africa and today the peach is thought to be the world's most widely cultivated fruit apart from the apple and orange.

There are two categories of peach: clingstone and freestone. As the names suggest they indicate the ease with which the flesh can be separated from the stone.

While there are those who suggest that the quality of a good peach makes it almost a crime to do other than eat them in their natural state, the peach has a range of culinary uses. They may be poached, used in pies or as the heart of that most popular of desserts, the peach melba. Then there are ice creams and jellies. They can also be stewed, grilled or flambéed.

With a sugar content of 9 per cent and a high vitamin A and C content, peaches are healthy. In fact, they are lower in calories than even apples and pears.

Starters
and
Savoury
Dishes

APRICOT SOUP

1lb/500g fresh apricots
2tbsp/30ml claret
Pinch of cinnamon
4ozs/125g caster sugar
1/2oz/13g arrowroot or cornflour
Oil for frying
Bread (diced)

Put the apricots in a saucepan with just enough water to cover and cook slowly until they are really soft. Remove the stones and press the fruit through a sieve or use a food processor to make a purée. Put purée in a saucepan, add the claret, sugar and cinnamon and dilute with sufficient water to your taste and quantity of soup required. Heat slowly until the sugar is dissolved and serve hot with diced fried bread.

APRICOT & MARROW SOUP (serves 3-4)

1lb/500g apricots (halved and stoned)
1lb/500g marrow
1oz/25g tapioca
Sugar and lemon juice to taste
1tbsp/15ml brandy

Prepare the marrow and cut into chunks. Place marrow, apricots and tapioca a saucepan with a little water and cook until quite soft. Pass the cooked mixture through a sieve and add the sugar and lemon juice to taste. Stir in the brandy and serve the soup hot.

APRICOT PORK CHOPS (serves 4)

4 pork chops (trimmed of fat)
8ozs/250g apricots (washed, halved and stoned)
2ozs/50g sultanas
oz/25g margarine
Half teaspoon curry powder
uice of 1 orange
tbsp/45ml stock or water
Watercress to garnish

eat the margarine in a frying pan and fry the chops quickly so they are
rowned on both sides. Place chops in an ovenproof dish.

hop the apricots but reserve four halves for garnishing. Put the chopped
pricots in the frying pan with the sultanas and curry powder, stir in the orange
ice and the stock or water and bring to the boil, stirring continuously.
heck for seasoning.

et oven at 180C/350F/Gas Mark 4.

ur the apricot sauce over the chops and cover the dish with a lid or foil.
ok chops for 45-50 minutes or until tender. When ready to serve place the
served halves on each chop and garnish with watercress. Serve with new
tatoes and peas.

CHERRY MOULD

ins dark red cherries
d water
sp/15ml gelatine
zs/250g cream cheese
sp/60ml pineapple juice
tercress

in the cherries and add water to the juice to give 16fl.ozs/500ml of liquid.
the cherries in a ring mould. Put a quarter of the liquid in a saucepan, add
gelatine and dissolve over a gentle heat. Add the rest of the liquid and stir
Pour over the cherries and leave in a cool place to set. Whip the cream
se and pineapple juice together until smooth. Remove the cherry mould
fill the centre with the cream cheese mixture. Garnish with watercress.

CHERRY SOUP

1lb 8ozs/750g cherries (stoned)
1pt/600ml cold water
Rind and juice of 1 small lemon
2"/5cm cinnamon stick
4ozs/100g caster sugar
1/4 pint/125ml hot water
2tbsp/30ml port (optional)

Rinse the cherries and put in a pan with the cold water. Thinly pare off the lemon rind and place in the pan with the cinnamon stick. Bring mixture to the boil and cook for 20 minutes until fruit is soft. Using a separate pan gently dissolve the sugar in the hot water, bring to the boil and simmer until the mixture becomes syrupy. Pour over the hot cherries, stir in and leave to cool. Then chill in a refrigerator for about 2 hours. Remove the lemon rind and cinnamon and taste the soup. Gradually add some of the squeezed lemon juic to your taste and the port (if desired). Serve chilled.

NB. Morello cherries are best for this recipe but if only sweet cherries are available they need shorter cooking time and less sugar.

STUFFED PRUNES

Can be used as a starter, part of a salad dish or for a buffet.

Cook prunes, halve and remove stone. Using either cream or cottage cheese mash with a fork and moisten with a little double cream. Season well with sa and cayenne pepper and if desired a few chopped seedless raisins or blanched almonds. Stuff the halved prunes with the cheese mixture and serve.

PRUNE AND APPLE STUFFING

8ozs/250g dried prunes
2ozs/50g seedless raisins
2ozs/50g fresh breadcrumbs
Pinch of salt
Half teaspoon sugar
egg yolk (beaten)
large cooking apples (peeled, cored and thinly sliced)

Cut the prunes into small pieces and place in a bowl with the remaining ingredients. Mix well. If mixture is a little dry add a little stock to moisten. Use with duck or pork.

SAUSAGE STUFFED PRUNES

ozs/250g large prunes
ozs/250g sausage meat
ozs/50g soft breadcrumbs
Salt & pepper to taste

Stuff the prunes generously with the sausage mixture and place in a lightly greased ovenproof dish. Cook for about 25 minutes or until well browned and serve as a main meal with vegetables or as a garnish with turkey.

PRUNES IN BACON

Cook prunes until tender but not too soft. Drain and remove stones.

Set oven at 200C/400F/Gas Mark 6.

Wrap each prune in halved slices of streaky bacon and push on to a skewer. Place in a shallow pan and bake for about 10-15 minutes until bacon is crisp. Remove from the skewers and serve with turkey, ham or pork.

To make a variation, stuff each prune with pickle or chutney before wrapping around with the bacon.

PRUNE SOUP

3ozs/75g sago
2pts/1200ml water
3ozs/75g sugar
8ozs/250g prunes
3ozs/75g raisins
4fl.ozs/125ml red currant juice or water
Almond paste

Put the sago and water in a large pan, bring to the boil and simmer until the sago is transparent. In a separate pan cook the prunes and raisins with the sugar. Add the cooked fruit to the first mixture with the currant juice or water, mix thoroughly and reheat. Serve soup hot with almond paste balls.

Creams,
Fools
and Ices

APRICOT CREAM

1 tin apricot halves
2ozs/50g caster sugar
1oz/25g gelatine
10fl.ozs/300ml milk
10fl.ozs/300ml thick cream (whipped)

Drain the apricots, reserve a few and cut the remainder into small pieces.
Put into a bowl and add two tablespoons/30ml of the drained apricot juice and
the caster sugar. Stir well. Dissolve the gelatine in the milk and add to the
apricot mixture with the cream mixing all the ingredients thoroughly. Pour into
a wetted mould and leave to set. When ready to serve remove the cream from
the mould and decorate with the reserved apricots and a little whipped cream.

SWEET APRICOTS

1 tin apricot halves
1tbsp/15ml honey
2ozs/50g ratafia wafers
5fl.ozs/150ml thick cream (whipped)
1oz/25g flaked almonds (toasted)

Drain the apricots and place the fruit and honey in a food processor or blend
and purée. Break the ratafia wafers into small pieces and fold into the whipp
cream with the apricot purée. Spoon into individual serving dishes and chill
before serving. Sprinkle over the toasted almonds when ready to serve.

CHERRY FOOL

b/500g ripe dark cherries
ozs/175g caster sugar
/2.5cm cinnamon stick
fl.ozs/150ml water
tbsp/30ml cherry brandy
)fl.ozs/300ml thick cream (whipped)

ash the cherries and remove the stones - using the tip of a potato peeler
akes the job easier. Put the cherries with the caster sugar, cinnamon stick and
ater in a pan, bring to the boil and simmer gently until the fruit is soft. Press
e fruit through a sieve to make a puree, check for sweetness and add a little
ore sugar, if needed. Add the brandy and stir well. Then fold in the whipped
eam to give a marbled effect and spoon into individual glasses to serve.
ep in a cool place until ready to serve.

HERRY DELIGHT (serves 4)

zs/250g ripe cherries
/600ml water
ce of 2 lemons
ated rind of 1 lemon
s/150g caster sugar
s/75g fine semolina
ggs
ozs/150ml thick cream (whipped)
w chopped nuts

h and stone the fruit, reserving 4 cherries with stalk to use for decoration.
the stoned cherries. Put the water, lemon juice, grated rind and 4ozs/125g
e sugar in a saucepan and heat slowly until the sugar has dissolved.
nkle the semolina on the top, and stirring continuously, cook very slowly until
mixture thickens - about 2 minutes. Leave to cool. Separate the eggs and
the yolks. Add yolks to the semolina mixture and then the whipped cream.
k the egg whites to a stiff froth and gradually add the remaining sugar.
into the cream mixture followed by the chopped cherries. Spoon into
dual serving dishes and chill. Decorate with the reserved cherries and a
kling of chopped nuts

ROSY DREAMS (serves 8)

4 large ripe peaches
4ozs/100g redcurrants (with stalks removed)
4tbsp/60ml water
2ozs/50g caster sugar
10fl.ozs/300ml thick cream (whipped)

Peel the peaches by pouring boiling water over them to split the skins. Remove the stones and cut the peaches into small chunks. Put the prepared currants in a small pan with the water and bring slowly to the boil. Remove from the heat when the skins begin to split and carefully stir in the sugar so as not to break up the currants. Leave to cool in a refrigerator. Mix the chopped peach and currants with juice together and add to the whipped cream. Spoon into individual glasses and serve with ratafia wafers or sponge fingers.

TROPICAL PEACH SUNDAE (serves 4)

1pt/600ml thick cream
4ozs/100g desiccated coconut
2ozs/50g icing sugar
1 egg
4ozs/100g plain chocolate (grated)
4 fresh peaches
Melba sauce (see recipe for Peach Melba on page 29)

Put the cream and coconut in a small saucepan and cook very slowly over a low heat for about 10 minutes. Stir in the sugar and leave to cool. Separate the eggs and when the cooked mixture is cool, beat in the egg yolk and pour into freezer tray. When half frozen, remove from the freezer and whisk. Whisk the egg white until stiff and fold into the cold mixture with the grated chocolate. Return mixture to the freezer until firm.

Peel the peaches, halve and remove the stones.

When ready to serve, place a scoop of the coconut ice in the bottom of a tall glass, top with two peach halves and the melba sauce. Decorate with whipped cream and toasted coconut flakes and serve with wafer biscuits.

ROYAL PEACHES

5 good ripe peaches
ozs/25g small strawberries
Ofl.ozs/300ml fresh double cream
ot/600ml milk
egg yolks
few drops of vanilla essence
ozs/125g caster sugar

ut the milk, egg yolks, sugar and vanilla essence in a saucepan. Bring to the
oil and cook until thickened. Leave to cool and then stand saucepan in a bowl
ice. Beat the fresh cream until firm. Peel peaches, halve and remove stones.
ut the chilled vanilla cream in the centre of a glass dish and arrange the peach
alves around it. Put some cream on each peach half and garnish with the
rawberries. Serve immediately.

UM LAYER (serves 6-8)

s/1kg ripe plums
zs/100g granulated sugar
zs/100g white breadcrumbs
zs/50g butter
ttle caster sugar
ozs/150ml double cream
g white (whisked)

oven at 180C/350F/Gas Mark 4.

e the plums and remove stones. Lightly grease a shallow ovenproof dish and
nkle over the granulated sugar. Cover and cook for about 35 minutes until
fruit is soft. Remove and leave to cool.

the breadcrumbs in the butter until brown, adding a little caster sugar.
ove the plums from the dish with a slotted spoon and put in a glass bowl in
rs with the toasted crumbs, finishing with a layer of crumbs. Whisk the
m until slightly thickened and fold in the whisked egg white. Spread over the
s and chill before serving.

PLUM RICE MOULD (serves 4-6)

Half pint/300ml water
5ozs/130g granulated sugar
1lb/500g plums (washed and stoned)
2ozs/50g pudding rice
1pt/600ml milk
Few drops of vanilla essence
½ oz/13g gelatine
1tbsp/15ml cold water
4fl.ozs/120ml thick cream
1 egg white

Put the water and sugar in a saucepan, bring to the boil and cook until syrup thickens a little. Add the plums and poach until they are tender. Set aside t cool. Wash the rice through a strainer and drain well. Put the milk in a saucepan, bring to the boil and add the rice. Cook gently until the rice is sof (about 30minutes), stirring occasionally to prevent sticking. When nearly all the milk has been absorbed remove from heat and stir in the sugar and vanill essence. Leave in a basin to cool.

Soak the gelatine in the tablespoon/15ml of cold water and then add 5 tablespoons/75ml of the plum syrup. Heat gently to dissolve the gelatine an stir carefully into the cooked rice. Whip the cream lightly and whisk the egg white until stiff and frothy; fold them both into the rice cream. Pour the mixture into a lightly oiled savarin mould, cover with foil and leave in a cool place to set. Drain the plums.

When ready to serve turn out the rice cream on to a serving dish and arrang the plums in the centre. If there are any plums over, press them through a strainer and add to the juice to make a sauce.

WHIPPED PRUNES

8ozs/250g stoned prunes
5ozs/150g yoghurt
2tbsp/30ml clear honey
10fl.ozs/300ml double cream
1oz/25g chopped walnuts

Place the prunes in a pan and just cover with water. Bring to the boil and simmer for about 15 minutes or until they are soft. Remove with a slotted spoon and put in a blender or food processor with 4fl.ozs/120ml of the liqui and blend until smooth. Leave to cool. Whip the cream and fold in the prur puree, yoghurt and honey and stir well. Spoon into individual glasses and sprinkle over the chopped walnuts. Serve immediately.

Soufflés and Mousses

APRICOT MOUSSE (serves 3-4)

12 soft apricots
10fl.ozs/300ml fresh cream
7ozs/200g caster sugar

Peel and stone the apricots and pass through a sieve or purée in a food processor. Whip the cream until really firm, add the sugar and then add the apricot purée. Stir well. Place in a freezer mould with a lid. Remove from the freezer about 15 minutes before serving.

APRICOT WHISK

Grated rind and juice of 2 oranges
1 tin of apricot halves in natural juice
5ozs/150g apricot yoghurt
1tbsp/15ml clear honey
A little demerara sugar (if desired)

Drain the apricots and put them in a blender or food processor to make a purée. Add the yoghurt, honey and orange juice and purée for a further minu‑
Pour into individual serving bowls and chill until ready to serve. Sprinkle over the grated orange rind and demerara sugar (if using) just before serving.

APRICOT SOUFFLÉ (serves 6-8)

lbs/1kg apricots
b/500g caster sugar
)fl.ozs/300ml water
 egg whites
z/25g caster sugar
bsp/15ml Kirsch (if desired)

alve and stone the apricots, put them in a pan with the sugar and water.
ack some of the stones (about 20), remove the kernals, dip into boiling water
1d peel them. Bring the apricots to the boil and then simmer until the fruit is
ansparent, adding the kernals after about 5 minutes into the cooking time.
emove pan from heat and allow to cool.

t oven at 180C/350F/Gas Mark 4.

ing a slotted spoon, remove the kernals from the cooked apricots and put
e apricots in a food processor to make a purée. Spread the purée in an
enproof dish. Whisk the egg whites and fold in the 1oz/25g of caster sugar
d Kirsch (if using). Pour over the fruit or stir in if you prefer. Bake for about
 minutes until the meringue is lightly browned. Serve immediately.

RIED APRICOT MOUSSE (serves 4-6)

500g dried apricots
ed rind and juice of 1 lemon
:s/75g sugar
gg whites
ted chocolate

k apricots overnight if necessary. Put in a pan with sufficient water just to
er dried fruit or use the soaking liquid, add the lemon rind and juice and
< until fruit is tender. Add the sugar, adjust to taste, and cook for a
her 5-10 minutes. Rub cooked fruit through a sieve or purée in a food
:essor and leave to cool.

the egg whites until really stiff and fold into the purée, a little at a time,
inuing to whisk. Pile into individual serving dishes and sprinkle over the
ed chocolate.

PEACH MOUSSE

6 ripe peaches
10fl.ozs/300ml double cream
7ozs/200g caster sugar

Pour boiling water over the peaches to loosen the skins. Peel, halve and stone the peaches and press through a fine sieve or purée in a food processor or blender. Whisk the cream until firm and add the sugar. Fold cream into the peach purée and spoon into a serving dish. Lightly chill before serving.

PEACH SOUFFLÉ

1 tin of peach halves
4 eggs (separated)
4ozs/100g caster sugar
1oz/25g butter (melted)
2ozs/50g flour
Pinch of salt
8fl.ozs/250ml milk
1tbsp/15ml brandy or sherry

Prepare a soufflé dish with a "collar". Drain the tinned peaches, reserving the syrup, cut the fruit into quarters and arrange at the bottom of the soufflé dish.

In a large bowl, beat the egg yolks and half the sugar until thick and yellow. Gradually add the melted butter, flour and salt, beating continuously. Put th milk in a small pan, bring to boiling point and pour over the egg yolk mixture. Stir thoroughly and leave to cool.

Set oven at 180C/350F/Gas Mark 4.

Whisk the egg whites until really firm and fold in the remaining sugar. Carefu fold into the milk and yolk mixture and add the brandy or sherry. Pour over t peaches and bake for about 30 minutes.

QUICK PEACH MOUSSE

tin of sliced peaches
tin of condensed milk
Water
tsp/5ml vanilla essence
Ofl.ozs/300ml double cream (whipped)

rain the peaches and purée in a blender or food processor. Pour the
ondensed milk into a saucepan, fill the empty tin up to two-thirds with water
nd dilute the condensed milk. Heat thoroughly until milk and water are
noroughly blended and leave to chill. Add the essence and fold in the whipped
ream and puréed peaches. Freeze in a covered container. When ready to use
move from freezer about 10 minutes before serving.

RUNE SOUFFLÉ

/500g stoned dried prunes
ittle water
ggs

t oven at 190C/375F/Gas Mark 5.

ew the prunes in a little water until soft. Remove with a slotted spoon into
od processor or blender and purée. Separate the eggs, beat the yolks and
d to the prune purée. Whisk the egg whites and fold lightly into the mixture.
r into a lightly buttered ovenproof dish and bake for about 10-15 minutes.
ve immediately.

NUT PRUNE SOUFFLÉ

8fl.ozs/250ml prune purée
4fl.ozs/125ml prune juice
4ozs/100g sugar
Pinch of salt
Quarter teaspoon of cinnamon
8fl.ozs/250ml boiling water
2ozs/50g flour
6tbsp/90ml cold water
2tbsp/30ml lemon juice
2 egg whites
3ozs/75g chopped walnuts

Put the prune purée, prune juice, sugar, salt, cinnamon and boiling water into a double saucepan and simmer over a low heat for 5 minutes, stirring continuously. Add the flour and cold water and continue to stir and cook until mixture becomes thick. Cook for a further 10 minutes and then add the lemon juice. Whisk the egg whites and carefully fold into the cooked mixture with the chopped walnuts. Pour final mixture into a dish and chill. Serve with whipped cream.

Ices
&
Frozen
Desserts

APRICOT ICE CREAM

4ozs/125g dried apricots
3 egg yolks
7ozs/220g sugar
8fl.ozs/250ml milk
8fl.ozs/250ml single cream

To decorate -
A little chopped dried apricot
Mint leaves

Put the apricots in a small saucepan, cover with cold water and cook over gentle heat until tender. Transfer the cooked apricots with liquid into a foc processor or blender and blend to a smooth purée. Put the egg yolks and sug. into a bowl and whisk until thick and creamy. Put the milk and cream in a sm. saucepan, heat to just under boiling point and then pour over the whiske mixture. Stand the bowl in a pan of simmering water and stir mixtu continuously for about 10 minutes when it should become creamy. Remove fro the heat. Pour the cooked mixture and the apricot purée into an ice crea container, cover and freeze. When ready to serve garnish as desired — a lit chopped dried apricot and mint leaves make an attractive presentation.

APRICOT ICE

12 fresh, ripe apricots
1pt/600ml cold water
8ozs/250g granulated sugar

Remove stones from the apricots and press through a sieve or purée in a foc processor. Put the water and sugar in a saucepan and heat gently while the sugar dissolves. Bring to the boil and test the syrup by pinching a drop of t liquid between finger and thumb. When a fine thread forms when trying to separate the two drops of liquid, it is ready to remove from the heat. This should make 1.5pints/900ml of syrup, but top up with a little water if below quantity. Stir in the apricot purée, leave the mixture to cool and then put ir freezer container. Place in freezer until ready to serve.

Alternatively you can use peaches for this recipe and you will need about 8 ripened fruit.

PEACH MELBA (serves 4)

good ripe peaches
ozs/50g granulated sugar
pint/300ml water
alf a vanilla pod
t/600ml vanilla ice cream
fl.ozs/150ml whipped double cream
or the melba sauce -

ozs/250g raspberries
ozs/50g icing sugar

t the sugar, water and vanilla pod in a pan, gradually heat until the sugar is
ssolved and then boil for about 3 minutes until it thickens. Peel, halve and
move stones from the peaches and poach gently in the syrup for about 10
nutes. Allow the peaches to cool in the syrup.

ake the melba sauce by pressing the raspberries through a sieve and beating
e icing sugar a little at a time as the purée thickens. Leave to chill.

en ready to serve, place a scoop of ice cream in each serving dish, arrange
o of the peach halves over it and coat each dish with a tablespoon/15ml of
e melba sauce. Decorate with a rosette of whipped cream.

ACH ICE CREAM - 1 (serves 6)

ozs/150ml whipping cream
ozs/200ml custard (cooled)
sp/30ml natural yoghurt
ell ripened peaches

decorate -
w thin peach slices
gs of mint

the cream until it is thick and fold in the cooled custard and yoghurt.
mixture into a shallow freezer container, cover and freeze for about an
. Remove from freezer and mash the mixture well. Return it to the freezer
a further 2 hours and then mash the iced mixture again. Remove the skins
stones from the peaches and place fruit in a food processor to purée.
the puréed peaches into the final mashed cream mixture and mix well.
ze for a further 2-3 hours until really firm. Before serving the ice cream
sfer to a refrigerator for about 1 1/2 hours or at room temperature for
t three-quarters of an hour. Garnish with peach slices and sprigs of fresh
if desired.

PEACH ICE CREAM - 2 (serves 4-6)

6 ripe peaches
8ozs/250g caster sugar
10fl.ozs/300ml fresh double cream (lightly whipped)

Peel peaches and remove stones. Place halves in a food processor or sieve and process to make a purée. Add the sugar and cream to the purée and put mixture in a covered freezer container. Freeze until ready to use.

Puddings

APRICOT CONDÉ

1lb/500g fresh apricots
4ozs/100g sugar
4tbsp/60ml water
1½ozs/40g pudding rice
1pt/600ml milk
2ozs/50g caster sugar
Vanilla pod or few drops of vanilla essence

Wash the apricots and remove the stones. Cook the apricots slowly until soft in the sugar and water. Put the rice, milk, caster sugar and vanilla in a double saucepan and cook slowly until soft.

Set oven at 180C/350F/Gas Mark 4.

Pour the cooked rice into a lightly greased ovenproof dish and put the cooked apricots in their syrup on top. Bake until the syrup caramelises. Remove from the oven and serve cold.

APRICOT SURPRISE

30fl.ozs/850ml milk
6ozs/175g granulated sugar
4ozs/100g plain flour
4ozs/100g chopped almonds
1lb/500g ripe apricots
6ozs/175g caster sugar
5fl.ozs/150ml water
Vanilla essence
1 egg white

Put the milk, granulated sugar and flour in a saucepan and cook slowly until mixture thickens, stirring continuously, and then add the chopped almonds. Wash the apricots, halve and remove the stones. Make a vanilla syrup with 4ozs/100g of the caster sugar, the water and vanilla essence and soak the apricot halves in this syrup for about an hour.

Set the oven at 180C/350F/Gas Mark 4.

Pour the almond mixture into a lightly greased ovenproof dish and cover with the soaked apricots. Whip the egg white until really firm and carefully fold in 1oz/25g of the remaining caster sugar. Spoon over the apricots and sprinkle over the last of the sugar. Brown in the oven for about 20-25 minutes and serve immediately.

APRICOT CROUTES

1lb/500g fresh apricots
4ozs/100g caster sugar
6tbsp/90ml water
sliced white or brown bread
butter

Wash the apricots, halve and remove the stones. Cook the apricots in the water and sugar until the fruit is really soft. Remove the crusts from the bread and cut with a shaped cutter if desired. Fry the slices in butter until golden brown and spread the compote over them. Arrange slices on a serving dish and pour the syrup over them. Serve immediately.

APRICOT SHAPE

2lbs/1kg fresh ripe apricots
1lb/500g granulated sugar
8ozs/250ml water
2 egg whites

Halve and stone the apricots and put in a saucepan with the sugar and water. Bring to the boil and cook until the fruit becomes transparent. Press the cooked fruit through a sieve and set aside to cool. Beat the egg whites until really firm and frothy and gradually add the apricot puree. Serve in individual serving dishes with a wafer or ratafia biscuit.

MISTY APRICOTS (serves 4)

12ozs/350g fresh ripe apricots
Pinch ground cinnamon
4tbsp/60ml water
2ozs/50g granulated sugar
1 egg white
Pinch of cream of tartar
2ozs/50g caster sugar

Cut the apricots in half, remove the stones and cut the halves into two or
three wedges. Put the apricots in a saucepan, add the cinnamon, water ar
sugar and cook over a low heat for about 5 minutes. Put the cooked apric
into a lightly greased ovenproof dish.

Set oven at 220C/425F/Gas Mark 7.

Whisk the egg white with the cream of tartar until firm and frothy and
gradually fold in the sugar. Spread the meringue over the apricots and coo
the oven for about 10 minutes when it should be golden brown.
Serve immediately.

LEMON AND APRICOT CRUMBLE (serves 4-6)

1lb/500g fresh ripe apricots
Grated rind and segments of 1 lemon
6ozs/175g granulated sugar
8ozs/250g plain flour
4ozs/125g margarine
4ozs/125g demerara sugar

Wash, halve and remove stones from the apricots. Put the prepared apric
a bowl with the lemon rind, segments (with pith removed) and granulated s
Mix well together. Sift the flour into another bowl, rub in the margarine un
the mixture resembles fine breadcrumbs and stir in the demerara sugar.

Set oven at 190C/375F/Gas Mark 5.

Lightly grease a shallow ovenproof pie dish and put half the crumble mixtur
the bottom. Lay the fruit mixture on top and then sprinkle over the remair
crumble mix, pressing down lightly. Bake for about 1 hour or until golden br
Serve hot or cold with custard or cream.

ICOT AND APPLE MERINGUE

00g fresh ripe apricots
/250g granulated sugar
zs/150ml water
/250g apple purée
g whites
/50g caster sugar

1, halve and remove stones from the apricots. Place in a saucepan with the ulated sugar and water, bring to the boil and cook until fruit becomes very and transparent. Press through a sieve or purée in a food processor. Mix apricot and apple purée and spoon into a lightly greased ovenproof dish.

oven at 220C/425F/Gas Mark 7.

k the egg whites until really firm and frothy, gradually adding 1oz/25g of aster sugar. Pile the meringue on the purée, sprinkle over the remaining r and bake for about 10 minutes. Serve immediately.

NCHY APRICOT CRUMBLE

00g fresh ripe apricots
p/60ml orange or grape juice
/125g granulated sugar
/60g plain flour
0g margarine
ge digestive biscuits

, halve and remove stones from the apricots. Put the fruit, juice and r in a saucepan and cook over a gentle heat for about 5 minutes. Sieve our into a bowl, cut the margarine into small pieces and rub into the flour. n the biscuits and stir into the flour and margarine mixture.

oven at 190C/375F/Gas Mark 5.
n the apricots into a lightly greased ovenproof dish and sprinkle over the it crumble mixture. Bake for about 15 minutes. Serve hot with custard or n.

APRICOT PANCAKE

6-8 apricots
2ozs/50g caster sugar
2 eggs
5ozs/140g plain flour
2tbsp/30ml rum
Pinch of salt
A little milk
Oil for frying

Set oven at 180C/350F/Gas Mark 4.

Wash, halve and stone the apricots. Beat the eggs, flour, rum and salt together adding sufficient milk to make a batter mix. Heat the oil in a large frying pan and when it is "smoking" pour in half the batter mix. When the pancake is cooked, transfer to a lightly greased tart dish. Place the halved apricots on top and sprinkle over the caster sugar, pour over the remaining butter, uncooked, and bake in the oven for 25-30 minutes. Serve hot with cream or creme fraiche.

INDIVIDUAL APRICOT PUDDINGS

3fl.ozs/500ml milk
ew drops of vanilla essence
ozs/75g caster sugar
ozs/100g semolina
z/25g butter or margarine
rated rind of 1 orange
eggs (separated)
ozs/250g ready-to-use dried apricots
l.ozs/140ml orange juice
l.ozs/175ml water
ramekin dishes

t oven at 190C/375F/Gas Mark 5.
t the milk, essence and sugar in a saucepan and heat gently until the sugar
s dissolved. Add the semolina, bring to the boil, simmer slowly and stir
quently for about 5 minutes until the mixture thickens. Remove from the
at and beat in the butter or margarine, orange rind and egg yolks. Whisk the
g whites until light and frothy and fold into the semolina mixture. Place
nekin dishes on a baking tin and grease and line the base of each one. Pour
al amounts of the mixture into each dish and bake for about 45 minutes.

le the puddings are cooking, put the apricots in a saucepan with the orange
e and water, bring to the boil and simmer gently for about half an hour or
il the apricots are very soft. Remove from heat, set aside to cool slightly
then purée the apricots in a food processor or blender. Add a little more
nge juice if the purée is too thick.

n ready to serve, turn out the puddings from the ramekin dishes (run a
e round the edge) on to a plate and spoon over the apricot sauce.

APRICOT FRITTERS

Pancake mix as for the apricot pancake on page 36
12 fresh ripe apricots
3ozs/75g caster sugar
1tbs/15ml rum
Oil for frying
A little extra caster sugar

Halve and stone the apricots. Mix the rum and sugar and spoon over the halved apricots. Leave to soak for about an hour. Prepare the pancake mix. Pour cooking oil into a large frying pan and heat until "smoking". Dip each apricot half in the batter mixture and put in the pan to fry golden brown. Remove with a slotted spoon, place on a warmed serving plate and sprinkle wit sugar. Serve immediately, very hot.

LUXURY APRICOT CONDÉ

2lbs/1kg apricots
1lb4ozs/600g caster sugar
8fl.ozs/250ml water
8ozs/250g rice
20fl.ozs/600ml milk
2 egg yolks
Crystallised fruit to decorate

Wash, halve and stone the apricots, put in a saucepan with 1lb/500g of the sugar and the water and cook until fruit becomes soft. Remove a few of the apricots and continue to cook the rest until they become transparent. Take the heat, put apricots in a food processor or blender and purée. Put the ric milk, vanilla essence and remaining sugar in a saucepan and cook slowly. Remove from heat, add the egg yolks and stir thoroughly. Then stir in the apricot purée.

Set oven at 190C/375F/Gas Mark 5.

Moisten an earthenware mould and place the reserved apricots in the centr pouring the apricot condé around them. Sprinkle over with sugar and place the oven just long enough to melt the sugar. Garnish with the crystallised fruit and serve.

APRICOT BAVAROISE

2 ripe apricots
Ofl.ozs/300ml fresh double cream
ot/600ml milk
ozs/125g sugar
 egg yolks
 few drops of vanilla essence

ut the milk, sugar, egg yolks and vanilla essence in a saucepan, heat slowly
ntil the sugar dissolves and then cook gently until mixture thickens slightly.
et aside to cool. Peel, halve and remove stones from the apricots and press
hrough a sieve or purée in a food processor. Beat the cream until firm, fold in
he apricot purée and then mix with the vanilla cream. Pour the mixture into a
ould and keep in freezer until ready to use. Remove from freezer at least half
n hour before serving.

3. Peaches will also do as an alternative for this recipe.

SUNRISE PUDDING

zs/175g margarine
zs/50g soft brown sugar
/500g halved, stoned and cooked apricots
zs/125g caster sugar
ggs
zs/125g self-raising flour
aspoon mixed spice

 2ozs/50g of the margarine in a bowl and cream with the brown sugar.
ead over the base of a 2pt/1.2l ovenproof dish. Remove the cooked apricots
n their syrup with a slotted spoon and arrange on the sugar base cut side

oven at 180C/350F/Gas Mark 4.

the remaining margarine in a bowl with the caster sugar and beat until light
fluffy. Add the eggs, one at a time and add half the flour. Beat thoroughly
then add the remaining flour, mixed spice and 1 tablespoon/15ml of the
cot syrup. Spread mixture over the apricots and bake for about an hour
n the sponge should be cooked. Turn out onto a warmed serving dish and
e with cream or creme fraiche.

APRICOT BROWN BETTY

4ozs/100g fresh breadcrumbs
2ozs/50g melted butter
1lb/500g cooked apricots
3ozs/75g brown sugar
A little grated nutmeg or
Half teaspoon cinnamon
Grated rind and juice of half a lemon
4fl.ozs/125ml hot water

Set oven at 180C/350F/Gas Mark 4.

Mix together the breadcrumbs and melted butter. Also mix together the suga
spices and lemon rind and juice. Lightly grease an ovenproof baking dish and
put a layer of the crumb mixture at the bottom. Spread over half the cooked
apricots and then a layer of the sugar mixture. Repeat the layers and finish
with a breadcrumb layer. Pour over the hot water and bake for 40 minutes,
covering the dish until the last 15 minutes, so the breadcrumbs do not brown
too quickly.

CHERRY OMELETTES

1lb/500g cherries
3ozs/75g plain flour
2 eggs
8fl.ozs/250ml cold milk
1tbsp/15ml kirsch
Pinch of salt
1oz/25g butter
3ozs/75g caster sugar

Beat together the flour, eggs, salt and kirsch in a basin for about 15 minutes
gradually add the milk and beat to a smooth paste. Leave to stand for abou
two hours. Wash the cherries and remove stalks and stones. Add to the
paste mixture. Melt some of the butter in a large frying pan and when it is h
pour in about one-third of the mixture. Cook both sides of the pancake until
golden brown and set aside in a warm place. Repeat the process twice more
using a third of the mixture each time and sprinkle generously with the cast
sugar. Serve very hot on their own or with cream.

CHERRY FRITTERS

About 1lb/500g dark cherries with stalks on
2ozs/50g plain flour
 egg (separated)
 tbsp/15ml cooking oil
8fl.ozs/250ml milk (lightly warmed)
 inch of salt
 tbsp/15ml rum
 aster sugar

ut the flour in a bowl, add the egg yolk, salt and oil and stir gently, gradually
dding the lightly warmed milk and then the rum. Ensure all is blended
noroughly and leave to stand for 2 hours. Whisk the egg white until really firm
nd frothy and fold into the batter mixture. Put the oil in a frying pan and
eat until "smoking". Tie about 6 cherry stalks with cherries together, dip in
ne paste and fry in the hot oil. When golden brown, place on a glass dish and
prinkle with caster sugar. Serve immediately.

HERRY SOUFFLÉ PUDDING

/500g dark red cherries
ozs/175g caster sugar
fl.ozs/300ml milk
zs/75g fresh white breadcrumbs
 ggs (separated)
 ated rind of half a lemon
 c oven at 180C/350F/Gas Mark 4.

nove stones from the cherries, place cherries in a saucepan and sprinkle over
/25g of the caster sugar. Leave on a low heat for about 3 minutes. Heat
 milk until just below boiling point and pour onto the breadcrumbs. Mix well
 after 5 minutes stir in the egg yolks, 1oz/25g of the caster sugar and
on rind. Remove the cherries from their pan with a slotted spoon and mix
 the breadcrumb mixture. Pour the mixture into a lightly greased ovenproof
 and stand the dish in a tin of hot water. Cook for about 35 minutes when
pudding should be just about set. Remove from the oven and turn down
heat to 150C/300F/Gas Mark 2.

 sk the egg whites until really firm and peak well and gradually fold in the
aining sugar. Pile onto the top of the pudding, dust with a little caster
 ar and leave for about 5 minutes. Then put pudding in the oven for a
 ner 30 minutes. Serve hot or cold with cream.

CHERRY COBBLER (serves 4)

1lb/500g dark red cherries
6ozs/175g sugar
1 egg (well beaten) or half ounce/15g flour

For the topping -
6ozs/175g plain flour
2tsp baking powder
Pinch of salt
4ozs/125g sugar
1 egg
4fl.ozs/120ml milk
4ozs/125g butter (melted)

Set oven at 400F/200C/Gas Mark 6.

Wash the cherries, remove stalks and stones, add the sugar and egg or flour and arrange in a well buttered deep pie dish.

To make the topping put the flour, baking powder, salt and sugar in a bowl and mix well. In a separate bowl beat together the egg, milk and melted butter and stir gently into the flour mixture. Pour mixture over the fruit and bake for 20-25 minutes when it should be brown and crusty. Serve hot with custard or cream.

DIPPED CHERRY PUDDING

6ozs/175g cherries with stalks on
4 eggs (weighed)
Self-raising flour (equal weight to the eggs)
Caster sugar (equal weight to the eggs)
2ozs/50g melted butter
Pinch of salt
A few drops of vanilla essence
Set oven at 150C/300F/Gas Mark 2.

Separate the eggs and cream the yolks with the caster sugar until the mixture is really light and smooth. Gradually add the flour and melted butter, stirring constantly, then add the salt and vanilla essence. Whisk the egg whites to stiff peaks and fold into the flour mixture. Lightly grease an ovenproof dish and pour in the paste. Place the stalked cherries in the mixture, cover dish with a piece of buttered paper and bake slowly for about an hour or until "springy" to the touch. Serve hot.

CHERRY TURNOVERS

lb/500g dark red cherries
-ozs/125g caster sugar
Sozs/250g plain flour
ozs/125g margarine, lard or shortening
-4tbsp/45-60 ml cold water

ift the flour and rub in the fats, using fingertips, until mixture resembles fine
readcrumbs. Make a well in the centre and add 3 tablespoons/45ml of the
old water and mix quickly with a knife. Add extra water if the dough is a little
ry. Knead the pastry lightly on a floured board until it is smooth, wrap in cling
m and place in a refrigerator for about half an hour. Wash cherries and
emove stalks and stones.

et oven at 200C/400F/Gas Mark 6.

oll out the pastry on a floured board to about ¼"/5mm thick and cut into
unds about 4"/10cm across. Heap the cherries tightly together in the centre
each round and sprinkle over the sugar. Dampen the edges of the pastry,
d them over and seal by pinching together with the fingers. Place on a
eased baking sheet and bake for about 20-30 minutes. Dredge with sugar
fore serving hot.

HERRY BREAD PUDDING (serves 6-8)

zs/250g cherries (with stalks and stones removed)
500g bread
ggs (beaten)
s/1.2l milk
sp/30ml rum
s/200g sugar

oven at 180C/350F/Gas Mark 4.

the bread in a basin. Heat the milk with the sugar and pour over the bread.
ve for 10 minutes until bread is well soaked and then press through a sieve.
the rum, eggs and cherries to the bread pulp and stir well. Pour mixture
a lightly greased baking dish, sprinkle a little sugar on top and bake for
ut an hour.

BAKED GREENGAGE PUDDING (serves 4)

1lb/500g greengages
A little water
4ozs/125g sugar

For the sponge -
3ozs/75g margarine
3ozs/75g caster sugar
2 eggs
4ozs/125g self-raising flour

Wash the greengages, halve and remove stones. Arrange fruit in the bottom of a lightly greased pie dish, sprinkle over the sugar and add a little water. Cream the margarine and sugar together until soft and light. Beat in the eggs gradually with the flour until the mixture is smooth.

Set oven at 190C/375F/Gas Mark 5.

Spread the sponge mixture evenly over the fruit and bake for about an hour, when the sponge should be light and springy. If the pudding is browning too quickly, reduce the heat for the last half hour. Serve hot with custard or cream.

Plums would also be ideal for this recipe.

QUICK BAKED PEACH PUDDING (serves 6)

2 medium tins peach halves or 1 large tin
5ozs/140g soft cheese
6tbsp/90ml natural yoghurt
1 egg
1oz/25g demerara sugar
2ozs/50g muesli

Drain the peaches and place in a lightly greased pie dish. Put the cheese, yoghurt, egg and sugar in a bowl and whisk together until smooth.

Set oven at 180C/350F/Gas Mark 4.

Spread the cheese mixture evenly over the fruit and sprinkle over the muesli. Bake for about 30 minutes and serve warm.

Tinned apricots could also be used for this recipe.

PEACH COBBLER (serves 6-8)

4-6 ripe peaches (skinned, halved and sliced)
4 tbsp/60ml orange juice
3 tbsp/45ml clear honey
4 ozs/125g plain flour
1/2 tsp/8ml baking powder
2 ozs/50g margarine
1oz/25g light brown sugar
5 tbsp/75ml milk
a few flaked almonds
icing sugar to dust

Put the prepared peaches, orange juice and honey in a lightly greased shallow baking dish, ensuring the peaches are well coated. Set aside. Put the flour and baking powder in a bowl, cut up the margarine and rub into the mixture until it is fine. Stir in the sugar and gradually add the milk until you have a soft dough. Lightly flour a pastry board and roll out the dough to a round, about 7/18cm in diameter, and cut into six or eight equal wedges.

Set oven at 220C/425F/Gas Mark 7.

Arrange the wedges on top of the fruit, brush with milk and sprinkle over the flaked almonds. Bake for about 20 minutes when the scone dough should be well risen and golden brown. Serve immediately, dusting the top with icing sugar.

Fresh apricots could also be used for this recipe.

PEACH BAVAROISE

4 fresh ripe peaches
1/2 ozs/300ml double cream
1pt/600ml milk
5 ozs/140g sugar
4 egg yolks (beaten)
a few drops of vanilla essence

Skin the peaches, remove stones and cut into quarters. Put into a food processor or pass through a sieve to make a purée. Heat the milk gently with the beaten egg yolks, sugar and vanilla essence until creamy and then pass through a sieve to ensure smoothness. Beat the cream until firm, stir into the peach purée and then mix into the vanilla cream. Pour the mixture into a freezer mould, cover and freeze until required.

SUNSET PEACHES (serves 6-8)

6-8 fresh ripe peaches
4ozs/125g granulated sugar
5fl.ozs/150ml water
1tbsp/15ml Kirsch
1pt/600ml milk
A few drops of vanilla essence
4ozs/125g plain flour
4ozs/125g caster sugar
3 egg yolks (beaten)
4ozs/125g butter
1tbsp/15ml apricot jam

Remove the skins from the peaches, halve and remove the stones. Make a syrup with the granulated sugar and water and poach the halved peaches in the syrup until soft. When cooked, stir in the Kirsch and leave to cool. Heat the milk in a saucepan with the vanilla essence and in a separate pan put the flour, caster sugar and egg yolks. Mix to a smooth paste and gradually add the boiling milk, stirring continuously. When the mixture boils, add the butter. Pour mixture into a round dish and, removing the cooked peaches with a slotted spoon, arrange them on the top. Stir the apricot jam into the syrup until smooth and then pour the sauce over the peaches. Serve warm or cold.

PEACH SHERRY TRIFLE (serves 6-8)

1 large tin peach halves (drained)
6 sponge cakes or 1 small jam swiss roll
2ozs/50g macaroons
10fl.ozs/300ml double cream (whipped)
4tbsp/60ml sweet sherry
1oz/25g caster sugar
A few ratafia biscuits

Slice the sponge cakes and arrange them at the bottom of the trifle dish with the macaroons and ratafias. Pour over the sherry and if not sufficiently moist add a little of the drained syrup. Boil up the remaining syrup from the peaches with the sugar and when nearly cold, pour over the cakes. Arrange the peaches on the top and cover with the whipped cream. Set aside in a cool place until ready to serve.

PEACH MILK PUDDING

b/500g pastry
 fresh ripe peaches
ozs/125g caster sugar
z/25g flour
fl.ozs/250ml milk
z/25g butter
 few drops of vanilla essence

et oven at 180C/350F/Gas Mark 4.

epare the pastry as for the French Plum Tart on page 69 Roll out the pastry
 a floured board about ¼"/5mm thick and lay in a shallow tart plate. Cover
e pastry with lightly buttered baking paper and weigh it down with dried
ans. Brush the rim with a little egg yolk and bake the pastry case "blind" for
out 45 minutes. Set aside to cool and remove the baking paper and beans.

move skins from the peaches, halve and remove stones and then cut into
arters. Arrange fruit on the baked pastry. To make the vanilla cream, put
 sugar and flour with a little milk in a saucepan and blend until smooth.
at slowly, gradually adding the milk and stirring continuously. Add the
ter and vanilla essence and continue to stir as the mixture thickens.
r over the fruit and put pudding in the oven for about 10 minutes to set and
wn.

ns may also be used for this recipe - use 1lb/500g wiped, halved and
ned.

PLUM CROUTE

1lb/500g fresh ripe plums
3-4 thick slices of bread (at least ½"/10cms thick)
4ozs/125g granulated sugar
2ozs/50g butter

Set oven at 180C/350F/Gas Mark 4.

Well grease a shallow ovenproof dish. Cut the bread, removing the crusts so it
fits in the base of the dish. Wipe the plums, cut in half and remove the stones
Place plums, cut side up and close together on the bread. Put a small knob of
butter in hollow of each plum with a little sugar. Bake for about 30-40
minutes until the plums are cooked, removing the dish from time to time to
sprinkle over more of the sugar until it is all used up. Serve hot or cold with
cream.

PLUM SURPRISE (serves 6)

1lb/500g plums (halved and stoned)
2ozs/50g soft cheese
2ozs/50g ground almonds
1oz/25g light brown sugar
2 eggs
4tbsp/60ml milk
2ozs/50g margarine
Icing sugar for dusting

Set oven at 200C/400F/Gas Mark 6.

Lightly grease an 8"/20cm round flan dish and arrange the plums in a circula
pattern. Beat the cheese, ground almonds and sugar together and then
gradually whisk in the eggs and milk. Melt the margarine and fold into the
batter mixture. Pour over the plums and bake for about 25-30 minutes unti
golden brown and set. Dust with the icing sugar and serve hot or cold.

PLUM CHARLOTTE (serves 4)

1lb/500g ripe plums
6ozs/175g stale fruit cake (crumbled)
2ozs/50g demerara sugar
1oz/25g butter

Set oven at 180C/350F/Gas Mark 4.

Wipe the plums, halve and remove stones, reserving 4 halves for decoration. Mix the sugar with the cake crumbs and arrange one-third of the mixture on the base of a lightly greased pie dish. Cover with half the prepared plums and then another third of the crumb mixture, followed by the remaining plums and the last of the crumb mixture. Dot the surface with the butter and bake for about 30 minutes when the fruit should be tender. Decorate the top with the reserved plums and serve with custard or cream.

PLUM PANCAKE

1lb/500g plums (wiped, halved and stoned)
4ozs/125g caster sugar
3 eggs (beaten)
3ozs/85g butter
4ozs/125g plain flour
1tbsp/15ml rum
pinch of salt
a little milk or water

Mix the eggs with the flour, add the rum, salt and milk and whisk to a smooth pancake batter. Put some of the butter in a frying pan and when hot, pour in half the batter mixture.

Set oven at 180C/350F/Gas Mark 4.

When golden brown both sides, lay the pancake in a lightly buttered tart tin. Place the plums on the cooked pancake, sprinkle over the sugar and cover with the remaining uncooked batter mixture. Bake for about 25-30 minutes and serve hot.

PLUM OMELETTE (serves 6)

2 bananas (peeled and thickly sliced)
1lb/500g plums (wiped, halved and stones removed)
4ozs/125g caster sugar
A few drops of vanilla essence
3 eggs (separated)
A little extra sugar for dusting

Set oven at 200C/400F/Gas Mark 6.

Put the bananas, prepared plums and 1oz/25g of the caster sugar in a lightly buttered ovenproof dish. Beat the egg yolks with the remaining sugar and vanilla essence until mixture is pale and thick. Whisk the egg whites until reall firm and lightly fold into the yolk mixture. Spoon over the fruit and bake for about 20 minutes until the top is golden brown and firm to touch. Serve immediately, dusted lightly with sugar.

LUXURY PLUM CONDÉ

2lbs/1kg plums
1lb4ozs/600g caster sugar
8fl.ozs/250ml water
8ozs/250g rice
20fl.ozs/600ml milk
2 egg yolks
Crystallised fruit to decorate

Wash, halve and stone the plums, put in a saucepan with 1lb/500g of the su and the water and cook until fruit becomes soft. Remove a few of the plum halves and continue to cook the rest until they become transparent. Take o the heat, put plums in a food processor or blender and purée. Put the rice, milk, vanilla essence and remaining sugar in a saucepan and cook slowly. Remove from heat, add the egg yolks and stir thoroughly. Then stir in the p purée.

Set oven at 190C/375F/Gas Mark 5.

Moisten an earthenware mould and place the reserved plums in the centre, pouring the plum condé around them. Sprinkle over with sugar and place in oven just long enough to melt the sugar. Garnish with the crystallised frui and serve.

LUM FRITTERS

bout 1lb/500g fresh ripe plums (wiped)
ozs/50g plain flour
egg (separated)
bsp/15ml cooking oil
fl.ozs/250ml milk (lightly warmed)
nch of salt
bsp/15ml rum
aster sugar

t the flour in a bowl, add the egg yolk, salt and oil and stir gently, gradually
ding the lightly warmed milk and then the rum. Ensure all is blended
oroughly and leave to stand for 2 hours. Whisk the egg white until really firm
d frothy and fold into the batter mixture. Put the oil in a frying pan and
at until "smoking". Using a slotted spoon, immerse the plums in the batter
d then into the hot oil until golden brown. Serve very hot sprinkled with
ster sugar.

UNE WHIP

s/250g dried prunes
s/50g caster sugar
gg whites
p/10ml lemon juice

the prunes in a pan and add sufficient water to just cover them. Leave to
k for a few hours and then cook them in the water until they are soft.
ove the stones and put cooked prunes through a sieve or food processor
ake a purée. Add the sugar to the purée and cook for about 5 minutes.
aside to cool.

oven at 150C/300F/Gas Mark 2.

k the egg whites until they are firm and frothy and gradually fold into the
d purée and then add the lemon juice. Spoon into a lightly butter
proof dish and bake for about 20 minutes. Serve cold with cream.

51

PRUNE CREAM

1lb/500g prunes
Rind of half a lemon
5fl.ozs/150ml claret or water
4ozs/125g granulated sugar
Half ounce/13g gelatine
1tbsp/15ml hot water
10fl.ozs/300ml whipped double cream
A few blanched almonds

Remove the stones from the prunes, crack them and add to the prunes. Put i
a saucepan with the lemon rind, claret or water and sugar and cook slowly unt
they are quite tender. Press through a sieve or put in a blender or food
processor, removing the stones and kernals first, to make a purée. Dissolve
the gelatine in the hot water and put in a small saucepan with the purée. Let
it come to the boil and pour into a ring mould. Leave to set and when ready t
serve, turn out onto a glass serving dish and fill the centre with the whipped
cream. Sprinkle over a few blanched almonds and serve.

PRUNES CONDÉ

1lb/500g dried prunes
12ozs/350g sugar
5fl.ozs/150ml water
7ozs/200g rice
1pt/600ml milk
2 egg yolks
Crystallised fruit to decorate

Remove stones from the prunes, put in a saucepan with 8ozs/250g of the
sugar and the water and cook until fruit becomes soft. Remove a few of the
prunes. Take off the heat, put remaining prunes in a food processor or blend
and purée. Put the rice, milk and remaining sugar in a saucepan and cook
slowly. Remove from heat, add the egg yolks and stir thoroughly. Then stir
the prune purée.

Set oven at 190C/375F/Gas Mark 5.

Moisten an earthenware mould and place the reserved prunes in the centre,
pouring the prune and rice mixture around them. Sprinkle over with sugar a
place in the oven just long enough to melt the sugar. Garnish with the
crystallised fruit and serve.

Pies, Flans & Cheesecakes

APRICOT FLAN (serves 6-8)

For the sweet pastry -
6ozs/170g plain flour
Pinch of salt
5ozs/140g butter
1oz/25g granulated sugar
1 egg yolk
2tbsp/30ml cold water

For the filling -
1lb/500g fresh ripe apricots
10fl.ozs/300ml water
3ozs/75g granulated sugar
Apricot Glaze (warmed) (see page 97)

To make the pastry, sift the flour and salt together, cut the butter into small pieces and add to the sifted flour. Rub the mixture with the fingertips until it resembles fine breadcrumbs. Stir in the sugar, mix the egg yolk with the cold water and pour into the flour mixture and mix quickly with a fork. Turn out on a lightly floured board and knead until smooth. Then wrap in cling film and pla in a refrigerator for about half an hour.

While the pastry is chilling prepare the apricot filling. Put the water and suga in a shallow pan, dissolve the sugar over a low heat and then bring to the boil. Cook rapidly for two minutes and then remove from the heat. Wash and halve the apricots and remove the stones. Place the halved apricots in a shallow p pour over the syrup and heat slowly until simmering gently and cook for about 15 minutes or until the fruit is soft. Leave to cool in the syrup.

Set the oven at 190C/375F/Gas Mark 5.

Roll out the pastry and line an 8"/20cm flan ring with the pastry. Bake blind for about 25-30 minutes. When cooked, remove carefully and leave on a cake rack to cool.

Brush the bottom and sides of the cooled flan case with the warmed apricot glaze and, using slotted spoon, lift the apricots out of their syrup and arrar in the flan case. Brush well with the glaze. Leave to cool before serving.

If you do not have any apricot glaze, use apricot jam warmed with a little of syrup.

FRENCH APRICOT TART (serves 6-8)

For the paste -

8ozs/250g self raising flour
5ozs/140g butter
oz/25g caster sugar
pinch of salt
egg yolk
fl.ozs/250ml double cream

For the filling -

5 good ripe apricots
ozs/140g sugar
little egg yolk

Mix all the paste ingredients thoroughly, wrap in cling film and leave in a cool place for about an hour. Wash, halve and stone the apricots.

Set the oven at 180C/350F/Gas Mark 4.

Roll out the paste and line a lightly greased shallow ovenproof dish with this. Arrange the halved apricots in the dish, overlapping and cut sides down and sprinkle over the sugar. Brush the edge of the paste with the little egg yolk. Bake for about three-quarters of an hour when the pastry should be golden brown and the apricots soft. Serve hot or cold.

CREAMY APRICOT CRUNCH

For the biscuit base -

8ozs/250g crushed ginger biscuits
3ozs/75g butter

For the filling -

1lb/500g fresh, ripe apricots
2ozs/50g granulated sugar
5fl.ozs/150ml water
5fl.ozs/150ml apple purée
5fl.ozs/150ml double cream (whipped)
2ozs/50g caster sugar
¼oz/8g gelatine
2tbsp/30ml hot water

Decoration -

A little whipped cream
1oz/25g toasted almonds

Melt the butter in a saucepan and stir in the crushed biscuits. Press mixture into an 8"/20cm pie plate and leave to cool.

Halve and remove stones from the apricots and cook in the sugar and water until soft. Remove 4 halves (to use for decoration) and purée the remaining cooked fruit. Mix the apricot and apple purées together and fold into the whipped cream with the sugar. Dissolve the gelatine in the hot water, leave to cool slightly and stir into the fruit mixture. When the mixture begins to set, pour into the biscuit base and leave to set. Decorate with the whipped cream toasted almonds and reserved apricots.

NUTTY CHERRY FLAN

For the flan pastry -
6ozs/170g plain flour
Pinch of salt
3ozs/75g caster sugar
3ozs/75g butter
3 egg yolks

For the nutty filling -
2ozs/50g unblanched almonds
2ozs/50g caster sugar
1oz/25g custard powder
5fl.ozs/150ml milk
5fl.ozs/150ml double cream (whipped)
1 teaspoon caster sugar

For the topping -
tin of dark cherries
glass of red wine
4tbsp/60ml redcurrant jelly
grated rind and juice of 1 orange

Put the flour and salt onto a pastry board and make a well in the middle. Add the other ingredients and gradually work them in using the fingertips. Knead the mixture lightly until it is smooth and then wrap it in cling film and chill for half an hour.

Put the almonds and sugar in a small heavy based pan and heat gently. When the sugar browns, stir the nuts carefully to toast thoroughly and then turn out onto an oiled tin and leave to cool. When they are cooled, crush with a rolling pin. Put the custard powder and milk in saucepan, mix to a paste and bring to the boil. Turn the sauce into a bowl and cover with cling film. When cool stir in the coated nuts.

Set the oven at 190C/375F/Gas Mark 5.

Roll out the pastry to line an 8"/20cm flan ring and bake blind for about 15 minutes. Remove carefully when cooked and leave to cool on a wire rack.

Drain the cherries. Put the wine into a pan and boil until it is reduced to half its quantity, add the redcurrant jelly, orange rind and juice and heat until the jelly has dissolved. Mix in the drained cherries, reserving a few for decoration. Put the flan case on a serving plate, spoon in the nut mixture and top with the cherries. Decorate with the reserved cherries. Serve cold.

OLD-FASHIONED CHERRY PIE (serves 6-8)

For the pastry -

12ozs/350g plain flour
Pinch of salt
7ozs/200g margarine or shortening or a mixture of the two
5-6tbsp/75-90ml cold water

For the cherry filling -

2lbs/1kg cherries
8ozs/250g caster sugar
1oz/25g plain flour

Put the flour and salt in a bowl, cut the fats into small pieces and rub into flour until the mixture resembles fine breadcrumbs. Make a well in the cent pour in about three-quarters of the water and mix quickly using a knife. Ac little extra water if needed. Turn out onto a floured board and knead lightly until smooth, then wrap in cling film and chill for about 30 minutes before using.

Wash the cherries and remove the stones.

Set oven at 190C/375F/Gas Mark 5.

Using two-thirds of the pastry, roll out and line a lightly greased pie dish. with the pitted cherries and sprinkle over the sugar and 1oz/25g of flour. R out the remaining pastry, dampen the edges with a little water and place o the top of the pie dish, sealing the edges well. Bake for about 40 minutes until golden brown. Remove from oven and sprinkle over a little caster suga Serve hot or cold with cream.

If you cannot get fresh cherries, use tinned ones. Drain the cherries, reserv about 4 tablespoons/60ml of the juice. Mix juice with 2ozs/50g caster su and 1oz/25g plain flour. Put the cherries in the pie dish and pour over the j Bake as above.

GLAZED CHERRY PIE

x 8"/20cm baked pastry case
tin dark cherries (drained)
ozs/50g sugar
teaspoon gelatine
)fl.ozs/300ml whipped double cream

1easure the drained juice from the cherries and make up to 8fl.ozs/250ml with
ater. Pour into a saucepan and add the sugar and gelatine. Heat gently until
1e gelatine dissolves. Arrange the cherries in the baked pastry case and pour
/er the syrup. Leave to cool. Cover with the whipped cream and serve
1mediately.

)PPED CHERRY PIE (serves 4-6)

/500g cherries (washed and stalks removed)
zs/75g plain flour
·ggs (beaten)
.ozs/250ml milk
zs/100g caster sugar

t oven at 190C/375F/Gas Mark 5.

the cherries in a lightly buttered ovenproof pie dish. Make a paste with the
·r, eggs, milk and sugar and lay over the cherries. Bake for about 25
utes or until golden brown and serve hot.

CHEATS CHERRY STRUDEL (serves 6-8)

6 sheets filo pastry
A little melted butter
2lb/1kg morello cherries
4ozs/125g cake crumbs
1 teaspoon cinnamon
8ozs/250g caster sugar
4ozs/125g ground almonds

Prepare the filling first. Put the cake crumbs, cinnamon, caster sugar and ground almonds in a bowl and mix together. Take stones out of the cherries, stir into the crumb mixture and set aside.

Set oven at 190C/375F/Gas Mark 5.

Lay the filo sheets out flat and brush each sheet with melted butter, carefully layering the sheets into a pile. Spread the cherry mixture evenly over the pastry and then carefully roll up the pastry away from you. Lightly grease a baking tray, place the strudel on the sheet and bake for 35-40 minutes until golden. Dust with icing sugar and serve hot or cold in slices.

LUXURY CHERRY CHEESECAKE (serves 6-8)

For the base -
6ozs/180g digestive biscuits
3ozs/75g butter
2 egg yolks

For the filling -
9ozs/250g cream cheese
3ozs/75g sifted icing sugar
½oz/13g powdered gelatine
2tbsp/30ml water
1z/25g chopped blanched almonds
2 egg whites

For the topping -
1lb/500g dark cherries
6tbsp/90ml redcurrant jelly
a little red food colouring (if desired)

Lightly grease a flan ring. Crush the biscuits in a polythene bag, melt the butter in a saucepan and stir in the crumbs and then the egg yolks. Turn the mixture into the flan ring and spread it evenly to the sides, using the back of a spoon. Leave to set in a cool place.

Put the cream cheese in a bowl and beat in the icing sugar. Dissolve the gelatine in the water over a gentle heat and stir into the cheese mixture with the almonds. Whisk the egg whites until they are really firm and fold into the mixture lightly. Spoon the filling over the biscuit base and return it to a refrigerator to set.

To prepare the topping, wash the cherries and remove stalks and stones. Arrange the cherries on the set cheese filling. Lightly warm the jelly until smooth and add the food colouring if desired. Spoon over the cherries just before serving.

FRENCH CHERRY TART (serves 6)

12ozs/350g dark cherries
8ozs/250g self-raising flour
5ozs/140g butter
3oz/75g caster sugar
Pinch of salt
1 egg yolk
8fl.ozs/250ml double cream

Mix together the flour, butter, 1oz/25g of the sugar, salt, egg yolk and cream t
make a paste, ensuring it is smooth. Cover with cling film and leave in a cool
place for about an hour. Wash cherries and remove stalks and stones.

Set oven at 180C/350F/Gas Mark 4.

Roll out the pastry on a floured board about ¼"/5mm thick and lay in a shallo
greased tart plate. Sprinkle half the remaining sugar and then the cherries c
the pastry base and top with the last of the sugar. Brush the edge of the
pastry with a little egg yolk and bake for about 45 minutes until golden browr

GREENGAGE PIE

Shortcrust pastry as for the Old Fashioned Cherry Pie (see page 58) using
about half the quantity.
1lb/500g greengages
6ozs/170g granulated sugar
A little water

Set oven at 225C/425F/Gas Mark 7.

Lightly grease a deep pie dish. Wash the greengages, halve and remove stor
Lay fruit in the pie dish, sprinkle over the sugar and add just a little water.
Cover with the shortcrust pastry topping, sealing the edges well and put in
pre-heated oven. After 20 minutes reduce the heat to 190C/375F/Gas Ma
for a further 15-20 minutes. Serve hot with custard or cream.

GREENGAGE TART

b/500g pastry

lb/1kg greengages

ozs/170g sugar

little egg yolk

repare the pastry as for the French Cherry Tart on page 62 Wash, halve and
move stones from the greengages.

et oven at 180C/350F/Gas Mark 4.

oll out the pastry on a floured board about ¼"/5mm thick and lay in a shallow
eased tart plate. Sprinkle half the sugar on the pastry base and lay the
eengages on top. Sprinkle over the remaining sugar and brush the edge of the
astry with a little egg yolk. Bake for about 45 minutes until golden brown.

EACH TART

500g pastry

O fresh ripe peaches

s/125g sugar

ttle egg yolk

are the pastry as for the French Cherry Tart on page 62 Peel peaches, halve
remove stones, then slice into quarters.

oven at 180C/350F/Gas Mark 4.

out the pastry on a floured board about ¼"/5mm thick and lay in a shallow
ased tart plate. Sprinkle half the sugar on the pastry base and arrange the
ed peaches on top. Sprinkle over the remaining sugar and brush the edge of
pastry with the egg yolk. Bake for about 45 minutes until golden brown.

ROSY PEACH TART

1lb/500g pastry
A little egg yolk
8-10 fresh ripe peaches
8ozs/250g red currant jelly

Set oven at 180C/350C/Gas Mark 4.

Prepare the pastry as for the French Cherry Tart on page 62 Roll out the
pastry on a floured board about ¼"/5mm thick and lay in a shallow tart plate.
Cover the pastry with lightly buttered baking paper and weigh it down with drie
beans. Brush the rim with a little egg yolk and bake the pastry case "blind" fo
about 45 minutes. Set aside to cool and remove the baking paper and beans.

Peel skins from the peaches, remove stones and slice fruit into quarters.
Arrange quartered fruit on the cooked pastry base. Lightly warm the red
currant jelly to make it smooth and pour over the peaches. Leave to cool and
then serve with cream or creme fraiche.

QUICK CRUNCHY PEACH PIE (serves 4-6)

8ozs/250g digestive biscuits
4ozs/125g butter or margarine
2ozs/50g caster sugar
4-6 fresh ripe peaches or
1 tin sliced peaches (drained)

Crush the biscuits in a polythene bag until fine. Melt the butter or margarin
a saucepan and stir in the biscuits and sugar. Mix thoroughly and press
mixture into a shallow dish. Put in a cool place to set. If using fresh peache
remove skins and stones and slice into quarters. Arrange sliced peaches or
the biscuit base and serve with ice cream or cream of your choice.

PEACH AND ALMOND FLAN (serves 6)

ozs/125g butter
ozs/125g caster sugar
rated rind of 1 lemon
small egg plus 1 egg yolk
ozs/175g plain flour
ozs/125g ground almonds
large ripe peaches
ozs/175g granulated sugar
fl.ozs/300ml water
ozs/175g cream cheese
bsp/30ml single cream
few blanched almonds & angelica to decorate

well together the butter, 3ozs/80g of the caster sugar, half the lemon rind
d eggs. Add the flour and three-quarters of the ground almonds to the
ter and sugar mixture, work in well and knead to a smooth paste. Wrap in
g film and chill for at least an hour.

oven at 180C/350F/Gas Mark 4.

out the pastry and line a lightly greased flan tin. Bake "blind" for about
an hour. Remove carefully from tin and leave to cool.

e the peaches and remove the stones. Dissolve the granulated sugar in
water and then poach the halved peaches until the skins come away easily
the fruit is soft but firm. Using a slotted spoon remove the peaches from
pan and set aside. Heat the syrup until it has slightly thickened and leave
ool. Beat the cream cheese with the remaining lemon rind, caster sugar,
nd almonds and the single cream. Spread mixture over the pastry base
arrange the peach halves on the top. Brush with the syrup glaze and
rate with the blanched almonds and angelica.

PEACH PIE

1 tin peaches

For the pastry -
12ozs/350g plain flour
Pinch of salt
6ozs/175g butter, margarine or lard (or an equal mixture of the two)
4-5tbsp/60-75ml cold water

Sift the flour into a mixing bowl with the salt and add the fat cut into small pieces. Rub lightly using fingertips until the mixture resembles fine breadcrumbs. Make a well in the centre and add 4 tablespoons/60ml of the cold water and mix quickly with a knife, adding a little more water if necessary to make a firm dough. Turn out on to a lightly floured board and knead until smooth. Wrap in cling film and chill for about an hour.

Set oven at 180C/350F/Gas Mark 4.

Using about two-thirds of the pastry, roll out and line a lightly greased 8"/20cm pie dish. Drain the peaches, mash them and spoon into the pie dish. Dampen the edges of the pastry. Roll out the remaining pastry and lay over the fruit, sealing the edges of the pie. Make a small cut in the top to let out steam. Bake for about 40-45 minutes or until golden brown. Remove from oven and sprinkle a little sugar over the top. Best served hot with cream or custard.

Dried peaches can also be used for this recipe - follow the instructions to prepare them before using for the pie.

AUSTRIAN PLUM DELIGHT

10ozs/300g packet of white bread mix
6fl.ozs/180ml warm water
1oz/25g butter (melted)
3ozs/75g ground almonds
2ozs/50g caster sugar
1 teaspoon mixed spice
1lb/500g dessert apples (peeled, cored and sliced)
2lbs/1kg plums (washed, halved and stoned)
6tbsp/90ml plum jam
1oz/25g flaked almonds

Add the warm water to the bread mix and knead the dough until smooth.
Cover and leave for 5 minutes. Knead the dough again and roll out to a
12"/30cm round on a lightly floured surface. Place in a 10"/25cm buttered flan
tin or on a baking sheet and brush the dough with the melted butter. Put the
ground almonds, caster sugar and mixed spice in a bowl, mix well and sprinkle
over the dough.

Set oven at 220C/425F/Gas Mark 7.

Arrange the apple slices and halved plums over the almond mixture and bake
for 25-30 minutes until the dough is well risen and the fruit is soft. Leave to
cool on a wire rack. Heat the plum jam and sieve so it is smooth and use to
glaze. Sprinkle over the flaked almonds and serve with cream or yoghurt.

CREAMY PLUM PIE

6ozs/175g short crust pastry (about half the quantity as for the Peach Pie on
page 66)
3tbsp/45ml condensed milk
1tbsp/15ml boiling water
26ozs/750g ripe plums

Set the oven at 190C/375F/Gas Mark 5.

Mix the milk and water together. Wash, halve and remove stones from the
plums and place in a lightly greased 2pt/1.5ml pie dish. Pour over the
sweetened milk mixture. Roll out the pastry and place over the fruit, sealing
the edges well. Brush with a little of the condensed milk and water and bake
for about 30 minutes or until golden brown. Serve hot with cream.

PLUM PASTIES (makes 4-6)

1lb/500g plums (washed, halved and stoned)
1x13ozs/370g frozen puff pastry
1 egg yolk (beaten)

Set oven at 200C/400F/Gas Mark 6.

Roll out the pastry on a lightly floured board and cut into rounds or squares. Lay the prepared plums in the centre of each round or square and sprinkle a little sugar over the top. Dampen the edges and fold the pastry over the fruit and press down to seal. Brush the tops with the egg yolk, place on a lightly buttered baking tray and bake for about 20-25 minutes when they should be risen and golden brown. Serve hot or cold with ice cream or cream.

PLUMS IN THE MIST

For the sponge flan -
2 eggs
3ozs/75g caster sugar
2ozs/50g self-raising flour (sifted)

For the filling -
10ozs/290g plums
4ozs/100g caster sugar
2 egg whites

5fl.ozs/150ml double cream (whipped)

Set oven at 190C/375F/Gas Mark 5.

Whisk the eggs and sugar together until thick and creamy, fold in the flour a bake in a well buttered and floured sponge flan tin for about 15 minutes. Remove from the tin and place on an ovenproof dish. Cut the plums in half, remove the stones and cook gently with 2ozs/50g of the caster sugar. Ren a few halves with a slotted spoon and mash or sieve the remaining cooked plums.

Set the oven at 180C/350F/Gas Mark 4.

Whisk the egg whites until really stiff and fold into the plum purée with the remaining sugar. Pour mixture into the flan case and set in the oven for 15 minutes. Decorate with the reserved plum halves and whipped cream just before serving.

FRENCH PLUM TART (serves 6)

12ozs/350g good ripe plums
9ozs/250g self-raising flour
5ozs/140g butter
3oz/75g caster sugar
pinch of salt
1 egg yolk
9 fl.ozs/250ml double cream

Mix together the flour, butter, 1oz/25g of the sugar, salt, egg yolk and cream to make a paste ensuring it is smooth. Cover with cling film and leave in a cool place for about an hour. Wash plums and remove the stones.

Set oven at 180C/350F/Gas Mark 4.

Roll out the pastry on a floured board about ¼"/5mm thick and lay in a shallow greased tart plate. Sprinkle half the remaining sugar on the pastry and then arrange the halved plums on top, sprinkling over the last of the sugar. Brush the edge of the pastry with a little egg yolk and bake for about 45 minutes until golden brown. Serve hot or cold.

PRUNE PIE (serves 4-6)

For the filling -

4ozs/100g dried prunes (stoned)
5fl.ozs/150ml cold water
2ozs/50g soft brown sugar
Knob of butter
A little lemon juice
Juice of half an orange
1oz/25g cornflour
2tbsp/cold water

For the pastry -

6tbsp/90ml corn oil
3tbsp/45ml iced water
10ozs/290g plain flour (sifted)
Pinch of salt
Grated rind of half an orange

Cut the stoned prunes into small pieces and soak in the cold water for about an hour. Put the prunes and water in a saucepan with the brown sugar, butter lemon and orange juices and cook gently for 5 minutes. Mix the cornflour with the cold water until smooth and add to the cooked prunes. Bring mixture to the boil, stirring continuously, and then set aside to cool.

To make the pastry, put the corn oil and water in a bowl and blend together using a fork. Gradually mix in the flour and salt with the oil and water, adding the grated orange rind with the last of the flour, until you have a light smooth dough. Add a little more flour if mixture is sticky.

Set oven at 200C/400F/Gas Mark 6.

Take half the dough and roll out on a generously floured board and line an 8"/20cm pie plate. Spread the filling on the pastry and dampen the edge. Roll out the remaining dough and cover the pie, sealing the edges well. Brush with milk and bake for 30-40 minutes until golden brown. Serve hot.

Fruit Desserts

BANANA AND APRICOT SALAD (serves 4)

Juice and finely grated rind of 1 orange
1oz/25g dark soft brown sugar
2tbsp/30ml rum
3 large bananas (about 1lb 8ozs/675g)
2ozs/50g ready-to-use apricots
Yoghurt or creme fraiche to serve

Measure squeezed orange juice and make up to 4tbsp/60ml if necessary. Put juice and rind in a frying pan with the sugar and rum and heat gently until the sugar is dissolved. Peel the bananas and cut into diagonal slices about 1/4"/6cm thick. Cut the apricots into strips and add to the pan with the bananas. Bring mixture to the boil, stirring gently until it has warmed through. Pour into individual serving dishes and serve warm with yoghurt or creme fraiche.

APRICOT BABAS

4fl.ozs/25ml lukewarm water
1 pack yeast
6ozs/200g plain flour
4 eggs
1oz/25g sugar
Pinch of salt
4ozs/125g butter (softened)
Apricot jam

Put the water in a mixing bowl, sprinkle over the yeast and leave to stand for minutes. Add 4ozs/125g of the flour and beat well with an egg beater or electric mixer. Add the eggs (one at a time) with the sugar, salt and remaining flour, beating continuously. Cover with a damp tea towel and leave to rise for about 45 minutes. Then gradually beat in the softened butter.

Well grease deep cupcake tins or dariol moulds. Put a tablespoon of batter i each tin. Cover and leave to stand for 10 minutes.

Set oven at 400F/200C/Gas Mark 6.

Bake babas until brown. Remove from moulds or tins and leave to cool. Cut small circular piece from the top of each cake, scoop out a small quantity of the inside and fill with apricot jam. Replace tops and serve.

APRICOTS IN SOUR CREAM

Using dried or canned apricots.

If using dried apricots, cook as instructed on packet. If using tinned apricots, drain off juice. Chop fruit and mix in the sour cream. Divide into individual serving dishes and sprinkle with brown sugar or chopped nuts.

ICED CREAMY APRICOTS (serves 6)

1lb/500g apricots (halved and stoned)
3ozs/75g caster sugar
½fl.ozs/300ml cold water
½fl.ozs/300ml double cream (lightly whipped)
2bsp/30ml rum

Put prepared apricots in a saucepan with the water and sugar, reserving 6 halves for decorating. Bring slowly to the boil and simmer for 30 minutes or until the apricots are soft enough to purée. Push cooked fruit through a sieve use a food processor and allow to cool. Fold the lightly whipped cream into the purée, pour into a freezer proof container and freeze for 2 hours.

Finely chop the reserved apricot halves, put in a small bowl and pour over the rum. Leave to soak for 2 hours. Remove the ice cream from the freezer, turn into a bowl and whisk for one minute. Fold in the soaked apricot pieces with the rum and return the ice cream to the freezer until solid.

MARSHMALLOW APRICOTS

8ozs/250g apricots (halved and stoned)
2tsp/10ml gelatine
4fl.ozs/125ml warm water
2 large eggs whites (whisked)
2ozs/50g caster sugar

Purée the apricots in a food processor or blender. Put the gelatine in a small bowl, pour over the warm water and stand bowl in a pan of simmering water to let the gelatine gradually dissolve. When it is clear and still hot, pour on to the whisked egg whites and whisk until the mixture resembles whipped cream. Fold in the sugar and the puréed apricots and whisk for a further 2-3 minutes. Serve in individual glasses.

APRICOT SUEDOISE (serves 6-8)

6ozs/175g caster sugar
15fl.ozs/375ml cold water
1 strip of lemon rind
2lbs/1kg apricots
12 whole blanched almonds
1oz/25g powdered gelatine
Juice of 1 lemon
2tbsp/30ml water

Put the sugar, water and lemon rind in a saucepan, heat gently while the sugar dissolves and then boil rapidly for about 15 minutes until the liquid is syrupy. Wash the apricots, halve and stone them and put in the sugar syrup. Bring back to the boil, cover the pan and leave to simmer gently until the fruit is tender. Using a slotted spoon remove 12 of the firmest halves and drain on kitchen paper. Place an almond in the hollow of each half and arrange cut side down in a 6"/15cm cake tin. Remove the lemon rind from the cooked mixture and push the remaining apricots and syrup through a sieve to make a puree.

Put the gelatine in a small bowl with the lemon juice and water, stand bowl in simmering water while the gelatine dissolves. Whisk the gelatine into the apricot purée and pour carefully over the apricot halves. Leave to set in a cool place.

When ready to serve, dip the cake tin briefly in hot water, put a plate over the top, turn upside down and remove tin. Serve with whipped cream or creme fraiche.

APRICOT SUEDOISE WITH MERINGUES

Make the suedoise as in the previous recipe and leave to set.

For the meringues -

2 egg whites
4ozs/125g caster sugar

Set the oven at 250F/130C/Gas Mark 1.

Whisk the egg whites until really stiff, add 1oz/25g of the sugar and whisk for another minute. Fold in the remaining sugar with a metal spoon. Spoon neat blobs of the meringue mixture on to a baking sheet lined with non-stick cooking paper. Bake in a slow oven for 45 minutes or until meringues are dry and crisp.

Turn out the suedoise as above, cover with whipped cream and decorate with the meringues. Serve immediately.

APRICOT CHARLOTTE

1lb/500g apricots (halved and stoned)
¼ pint/150ml water
2ozs/50g granulated sugar
2ozs/50g caster sugar
½oz/13g gelatine
6 tbsp/90ml water
½ fl.ozs/300ml double cream (whipped)

To serve -
quarter pint/150ml double cream (whipped)
1 packet of wafer biscuits

Put the water and granulated sugar in a saucepan, heat gently until the sugar has dissolved and bring to the boil. Add the apricots and poach in the syrup until tender. Remove fruit with a slotted spoon, keeping back 6 halves, and reserve the syrup.

Press the remaining apricots through a sieve to make a purée. Measure the purée and make up to 15fl.ozs/450ml with the syrup, stir in the caster sugar. Soak the gelatine in 6 tablespoons/90ml of water and then dissolve over a gentle heat. Add to the apricot purée. Pour into a plastic bowl, stand bowl in a bowl of iced water and stir mixture until it begins to thicken. Fold in the cream and pour into a prepared mould. Cover and leave in a cool place for at least 2 hours when it should be set.

When ready to serve, turn out the charlotte, spread cream on the biscuits and arrange overlapping round the sides of the charlotte. Decorate top with reserved apricot halves and piped cream.

APRICOTS WITH KIRSCH

12 fresh apricots
8ozs/250g sugar
1 small glass of kirsch

Halve and stone the apricots. Put in a pan with the sugar and a little water and cook until soft but not mushy. Crack the stones, dip the kernels in boiling water and peel them. Arrange the fruit on a glass dish and stick the kernels in it. Pour over the kirsch and serve.

APRICOT BASKET WITH STRAWBERRIES

9 firm apricots
8ozs/250g small strawberries
8ozs/250g caster sugar
10fl.ozs/300ml double cream

Halve and stone the apricots. Whip the cream with the sugar until really firm and put half of it in the centre of a glass dish. Arrange the apricot halves around the cream, cut side up and fill with the strawberries. Decorate with the whipped cream and serve chilled.

NB. Raspberries may also be used for this recipe.

BAKED APRICOTS

Halve and stone the apricots, place in a dish and cover with sugar. Leave for 12 hours or overnight.

Set oven at 350F/180C/Gas Mark 4.

Place soaked apricots in a flame proof dish and bake for about 20 minutes. Leave to cool and serve with whipped cream.

APRICOT COMPOTE

2lbs/1kg apricots
1lb/500g sugar
½ fl.oz/300ml water

Halve and stone the apricots and place in a pan with the sugar and water. Bring to the boil and cook rapidly until the fruit become transparent. Crack about 20 of the stones, remove the kernals, dip in boiling water and peel them. Add to the apricots just before removing from heat. Serve cold with ice cream.

CHERRY BAKE (serves 6)

1lb 8ozs/750g cherries (stoned)
3 large eggs (beaten)
2ozs/50g plain flour
Pinch of salt
4ozs/125g caster sugar
15fl.ozs/450ml lukewarm milk
1oz/25g butter

Set oven at 425F/220C/Gas Mark 7.

Wash the cherries and dry gently on kitchen paper. Whisk the eggs and flour together with the salt and stir in half the sugar. Pour in the lukewarm milk, whisking continuously. Pour the batter mix into a lightly greased shallow ovenproof dish and sprinkle over the cherries. Bake for about 25 minutes or until the cherries have risen to the top and the batter is set and golden. Sprinkle over the remaining sugar and serve warm.

CHERRY COMPOTE

1lb/500g dark red cherries
8ozs/250g sweet almonds (blanched and split in half)
10fl.ozs/300ml water
12ozs/340g caster sugar
1tbsp/15ml Kirsch

Remove stalks and stones from the cherries and mix with the almonds. Mak thick syrup by heating the water and sugar together, bringing to the boil and simmering until it thickens. Set aside to cool and then add the Kirsch. Put the prepared cherries in a glass dish and pour over the syrup. Serve with sponge cakes.

WHIPPED CHERRIES

2lbs/1kg cherries (washed and stoned)
8ozs/250g caster sugar
4fl.ozs/125ml water
1oz/25g powdered gelatine
2tbsp/30ml cold water
4 egg whites
pinch of salt

Put the sugar and water in a pan, heat slowly while the sugar dissolves and then boil rapidly for about 10 minutes to get a syrup. Add the prepared cherries and simmer for 3-5 minutes. Drain the fruit. Mix the gelatine with the cold water and then pour over the cherry juice. You should have about 10fl.ozs/300ml of liquid. Allow to cool and place the liquid in a refrigerator to set. Remove from the refrigerator and whip up chilled liquid with an egg beater or blender until it is fluffy.

Whisk the egg whites with the salt until they are stiff and fold into the whipped sauce. Moisten the inside of a jelly mould or soufflé dish and pour in a little of the whipped mixture. Arrange a layer of cherries on top and another layer of the mixture. Continue with layers finishing with the whipped mixture. Chill until the mould is set. When ready to serve, plunge the mould briefly into hot water before turning out on a serving dish. Decorate with a few reserved cherries and angelica strips.

. A variety of other fruits can be used for this recipe.

STEWED CHERRIES

2lb/1kg cherries
10ozs/285g caster sugar

Remove the stalks and put the cherries in a pan of boiling water. When they rise to the surface, remove them with a slotted spoon and place in a glass dish. Sprinkle over the sugar and leave for at least 24 hours. If dish is kept in a cool place the cherries will keep for 4-5 days.

79

POACHED CHERRIES

1lb/500g dark cherries (washed and stones removed)
4ozs/125g demerara sugar
Juice of 1 lemon

Set oven at 350F/180C/Gas Mark 4.

Put the prepared cherries in an ovenproof dish with the sugar and lemon juice. Put dish in the oven and cook cherries until they are tender. The juice will be deep red and the cherries delicious served either hot or cold.

MIXED FRUIT JELLY

8ozs/250g cherries (washed and stoned)
1lb/500g raspberries
8ozs/250g red or blackcurrants
1pt/600ml water
2ozs/50g fine sago
6ozs/150g granulated sugar
Clotted cream to serve

Crack the cherry kernals and remove stalks from the currants. Put all the fru with the kernals in a pan with the water. Bring to the boil, cover and simmer gently until the currants split and release their juices. Put the cooked fruit through a sieve and return the purée to the pan with the sago and sugar. Boil mixture carefully for about 3-5 minutes when the sago should be cooked stirring continuously to ensure it does not stick to the pan. Pour into a wet mould and leave to cool. When ready to serve, turn out jelly on to a serving dish and serve with the clotted cream.

UTTERED CHERRIES

ɔ/500g cherries (washed, halved and stoned)
slices of bread
ɔzs/140g butter
ɔzs/75g caster sugar

ɛt oven at 325F/170C/Gas Mark 3

y the slices of bread in half the butter and lay them on a baking sheet.
t the prepared cherries on the bread and dot the remaining butter over the
rface of the fruit. Sprinke over the sugar and bake for 20-25 minutes.
rve hot.

IERRY SPECIAL

500g sweet black cherries (washed and stoned)
ːs/125g sugar
ttle water
sp/30ml Kirsch
ɔzs/150ml double cream
ɛw macaroon biscuits
ɛw chopped nuts (for decoration if desired)

k the cherries gently in the water and sugar so they remain whole. Allow to
and add the kirsch. Using individual glass dessert dishes, put a macaroon
ıe bottom of each dish and spoon over the cooked cherries. Whip the cream
very firm and put some on the top of each glass. Decorate with a few
ɔped nuts.

CHERRIES WITH MACAROONS & ORANGE CREAM

1lb 8ozs/750g cherry compote (see recipe on page 78)

For the macaroons -
4ozs/125g ground almonds
8ozs/250g caster sugar
2 egg whites
Few drops of vanilla or almond essence
½oz/13g plain flour

For the orange cream -
4 sugar lumps
1 orange
10fl.ozs/300ml whipped double cream

Set the oven at 325F/170C/Gas Mark 3.

To make the macaroons, mix the ground almonds and sugar well together. Break the egg whites with a fork and gradually add to the almond mixture, blending thoroughly. Add the essence and leave the mixture to rest for about 10 minutes. Put the mixture into a forcing bag and, using a plain nozzle, pipe small flat rounds onto a lightly greased and floured baking sheet. Bake for 12-15 minutes until macaroons are well cracked and light in colour. Do not allow brown or overbake. Remove from oven and leave on a wire rack to cool.

Rub the sugar lumps over the orange to absorb the oils from the rind and then crush them in a bowl. Strain the juice from the orange, add to the crushed sugar lumps and then stir into the whipped cream.

Using a large glass serving dish, arrange a layer of macaroons and then the cherry compote, using a slotted spoon to strain off some of the juice. Continue with layers of macaroons and cherries finishing with a layer of crushed macaroons. Spoon over the orange cream and leave in a cool place a short while before serving.

GREENGAGE COMPOTE

2lbs/1kg greengages
10ozs/285g granulated sugar
9fl.ozs/250ml water

Halve the greengages and remove the stones. Put the sugar and water in a pan, bring to the boil slowly while the sugar dissolves and then simmer for about 10 minutes to make a syrup. Add the prepared greengages and boil again for 10 minutes. Remove the fruit with a slotted spoon and place on a serving dish. Return the pan with the syrup to the heat and boil briskly until it becomes very thick. Pour over the fruit and serve hot or cold.

GREENGAGES WITH KIRSCH (serves 6-8)

2lbs/1kg greengages (washed, halved and stoned)
10ozs/285g sugar
9ozs/250ml water
2tsp/30ml kirsch

Make a syrup by boiling the water and sugar together for 10 minutes. Add the prepared fruit and continue to boil for another 10 minutes. Remove the fruit from the pan with a slotted spoon and arrange on a serving dish. Return the pan with the syrup to the heat and cook it rapidly until it thickens. Pour it over the fruit and add the kirsch whilst it is all hot. Serve warm.

SPICY PEACHES (serves 6)

16fl.ozs/500ml red wine
2 cinnamon sticks
3 whole cloves
Finely grated rind and juice of 1 orange
2ozs/50g caster sugar
2fl.oz/50ml water
6 good ripe peaches

Put the red wine, spices, orange rind and sugar in a saucepan and heat gently
for about 5 minutes until the sugar is dissolved. Pour spiced wine into a
shallow glass serving bowl. Wash the peaches, cut them in half to remove the
stones and then cut fruit into quarters. Place peaches skin side up in the
spiced wine and spoon over the fruit. Leave to soak for about 4 hours or
overnight, stirring occasionally. Serve from the main dish or spoon into
invididual serving bowls. Serve with creme fraiche or fresh cream.

Apricots are equally delicious for this recipe.

PEACHES IN WHITE WINE (serves 8)

8 good firm peaches
Half pint/300ml dry white wine
3ozs/75g caster sugar
2ozs/50g sugar lumps
1 large lemon
2tsp/10ml arrowroot

Set oven at 350F/180C/Gas Mark 4.

To skin the peaches, pour boiling water over them to split the skins and then
carefully peel them away. Place skinned fruit in an ovenproof dish and pour
the wine and water and stir in the sugar. Cover dish with a lid or foil and ba
for about 30 minutes. While the peaches are cooking, rub the sugar lumps
the lemon to absorb the oil. Squeeze the juice out of the lemon and strain.
Using a slotted spoon, remove the peaches and arrange on a serving dish.
small pan blend the arrowroot with a little cold water and add the hot syru
stirring continuously. Heat gently until mixture thickens and clears and st
the lemon juice. Pour liquid over the peaches. Crush the sugar lumps and
sprinkle over the peaches. Serve immediately.

SPARKLING PEACHES

firm ripe peaches
zs/125g caster sugar
3 glasses of champagne or sparkling white wine

be the peaches, halve and remove stones. Arrange in a glass dish, cut side
and sprinkle over the sugar. Just before serving, pour over the champagne
sparkling white wine.

ernatively, brandy may be used if preferred.

UFFED PEACHES

v 1 peach per person
ter
vn sugar   } in equal quantities
onut

oven at 375F/190C/Gas Mark 5.

e and stone the peaches and place in an ovenproof dish, cut side up.
he butter, sugar and coconut and fill the centres of the halved peaches.
for about 30 minutes and serve immediately.

PEACH SURPRISE (serves 4)

4 good ripe peaches
12 ratafia wafers
1tbsp/15ml Grand Marnier or liqueur of your choice
Grated rind and juice of half an orange
1oz/25g caster sugar
5fl.ozs/150ml double cream

Peel the peaches by pouring boiling water over them to split the skins so they peel away easily, and then halve and remove stones. Crumble the wafers into small dish and pour the liqueur over the crumbs. Put the soaked crumbs into the hollow of the halved peaches and then push the peaches back together. Put each peach in an individual serving dish.

Mix the grated orange rind and juice with the sugar and stir until sugar is dissolved. Whip the cream and as it thickens, add the orange syrup. Spoon over the peaches and leave in a cool place until ready to serve.

PEACH MOULD (serves 4)

5 peaches
A few cherries
3tsp/15ml gelatine
3tbsp/45ml hot water
Half pint/300ml milk
1oz/25g sugar
Almond essence
Green food colouring

Peel and stone the peaches and cut flesh into small pieces. Remove stones from cherries and arrange the fruit in a plain mould or tin. Dissolve the gelatine in hot water and add gradually to the milk. Stir in the sugar and essence and colour with the food colouring. Pour carefully over the fruit and place in a refrigerator to set.

CHES WITH LEMON

aches
/140g caster sugar
e lemon

he peaches, halve and remove stone. Place in a glass serving dish, sprinkle
the sugar and the juice from the lemon. Leave to stand for about 2 hours
e serving.

natively you may wish to substitute the lemon juice with 3
spoons/45ml of Kirsch.

CH COBBLER (serves 4-6)

ipe peaches (peeled, halved and stones removed)
/170g self raising flour
 salt
/75g caster sugar
(well beaten)
/130ml milk
/100g melted butter

ven at 375F/190C/Gas Mark 5.

ige the prepared peaches in a lightly greased ovenproof dish. Sift the
 salt and sugar together into a bowl. Mix the beaten egg with the milk and
d butter and stir gently into the flour. Beat well and pour over the fruit.
 for about 20-25 minutes until brown and crusty. Serve hot with custard
am.

ROSY PEACHES

8 good ripe peaches
1lb/500kg jar of red currant jelly

Peel and halve the peaches and remove the stones. Put the jelly in a pan to heat and add the prepared fruit. Bring to the boil and cook for 5 minutes. Pour into a glass serving dish and serve cold.

RIVIERA PEACHES

Allow 1 peach per person
Strawberries or raspberries sieved
Sugar to taste
A little lemon juice
Cointreau

Peel peaches and leave whole. Mix the sieved strawberries or raspberries or a mixture of both and sweeten to taste with the sugar. Add lemon juice and Cointreau and pour over the peaches. Leave for about 2 hours before serving

BAKED PEACHES

Allow 1 peach per person
A mixture in equal quantities of chopped nuts, fruits or macaroon crumbs
A little sherry or brandy

Set oven at 350F/180C/Gas Mark 4.

Peel, halve and remove stones from peaches and arrange in a lightly greased ovenproof dish, cut side up. Fill each cavity with the nut and fruit mixture. Bake for about 20 minutes and serve warm, pouring over a little sherry or brandy just before serving. Serve with whipped cream or creme fraiche.

Alternatively a mixture of sugar, butter with lemon juice and a little grated nutmeg can be used to fill each peach half.

PEACHES FLAMBÉ

A can of halved peaches
Maple syrup
Brandy

Set oven at 350F/180C/Gas Mark 4.

Arrange canned halved peaches cut side down in a shallow ovenproof dish and spoon over a little of the syrup. Pour over a generous quantity of maple syrup. Bake for about half an hour. When ready to serve, pour over the brandy and light with a match. Serve immediately.

SAUCY PEACHES (serves 6)

1lb/500g blackcurrants (stalks removed)
4ozs/125g caster sugar
8fl.ozs/250ml water
Grated rind and juice of 1 orange
6 good ripe peaches

Peel the peaches and leave whole. Put the blackcurrants, sugar and water in a pan and cook gently until the fruit is soft, stirring occasionally. Press cooked fruit through a sieve to extract as much pulp as possible and mix the orange rind and juice into the puree. Place the prepared peaches in a serving bowl and pour over the blackcurrant puree. Leave to chill and serve with cream or creme fraiche.

PEACH COMPOTE

10 fresh ripe peaches
10ozs/285g granulated sugar
16fl.ozs/500ml water
Peel the peaches, halve and remove the stones. Put the sugar and water in a pan, heat slowly while the sugar dissolves and then simmer until the liquid thickens. Add the prepared peaches and poach for about 5 minutes.
Pour onto a glass dish and allow to cool before serving.

QUICK PEACH BRULEE (serves 6)

6 fresh peaches
2tbsp/30ml Cointreau
10fl.oz/290ml whipped double cream
4ozs/125g soft brown sugar

Remove the skins from the peaches, halve and take out the stones. Place peaches, cut side down, in a shallow ovenproof dish and spoon over the Cointreau. Spread the cream over the top to cover completely and sprinkle with the sugar. Place dish under a hot grill for about 3 minutes when the sugar should have caramelized. Leave to cool before serving.

PEACH MERINGUE

nned peach halves
egg whites
ozs/50g caster sugar
sp/5ml lemon juice
nch of salt

et oven at 425F/220C/Gas Mark 7.

ain peaches and arrange in an ovenproof dish. Whisk egg whites until they rm soft peaks and gradually beat in the sugar, lemon juice and salt. pread evenly over the peaches and brown in the oven for about ten minutes. rve immediately.

ALMOND PEACHES (serves 4)

4 firm fresh peaches
2ozs/50g ground almonds
3tbsp/45ml red currant jelly
Few drops of lemon juice

Wash the peaches, halve and remove the stones and place cut side up in a
shallow ovenproof dish. Mix the ground almonds with half the redcurrant jelly
and lemon juice and spread over the peaches, filling the cavities. Place under a
preheated grill and cook until the almond mixture is brown. Warm the remaining
red currant jelly and spoon over the grilled peaches. Serve warm or leave to
cool.

CHILLED PEACHES

Tin of peach halves or use fresh peaches washed, halved and stoned.
Mix together some whipped double cream, chopped nuts, glacé cherries, a little
sugar and a tablespoonful of your favourite liqueur. Place halved peaches in a
dish, cut side up, cover with the cream mixture and frost lightly in the freezer
before serving.

HONEYED PEACHES

4 firm peaches (peeled, stoned and quartered)
tbsp/15ml clear honey
6tbsp/90ml orange juice

Put the honey and orange juice in a pan and heat slowly to dissolve the honey.
Add the peaches, cover the pan and cook over a gentle heat for about 8
minutes. Serve either hot or cold.

LUMS WITH KIRSCH

2s/1kg plums
ozs/290g sugar
l.oz/250ml water
bsp/30ml Kirsch

lve the plums and remove stones. Place in a pan with the water and sugar
d cook gently until the fruit softens. Remove fruit from pan with a slotted
oon and put in a glass dish. Continue to cook the juice until it becomes
cker. Pour the kirsch over the fruit and then add the cooked juice.
ve hot.

an alternative try brandy.

PLUM COMPOTE

2lbs/1kg plums
8ozs/250g granulated sugar
8fl.ozs/250ml water

Wash, halve and remove stones from the plums and put into a saucepan with the sugar and water. When fruit is soft, remove from the pan with a slotted spoon and put in a glass dish. Return the juice to the heat, simmer until it becomes thick and pour over the cooked plums. Serve hot or cold.

DRIED FRUIT BRULEE

6ozs/175g dried apple rings
2ozs/50g dried prunes (ready to use variety)
2ozs/50g dried apricots (ready to use variety)
20fl.ozs/600ml water
Grated rind and juice of 1 orange
Grated rind and juice of 1 lemon
Pinch of ground cloves and nutmeg
1 cinnamon stick
5fl.ozs/150ml whipped double cream
2tbsp/30ml clear honey
1oz/25g demerara sugar

Place all the fruit in a saucepan with the water, add the grated orange and lemon rind, the orange juice, 1 tablespoon/15ml of the lemon juice and the spices. Bring to the boil and simmer gently for about 10 minutes when the fr should be quite tender. Mix the cream and honey. Drain the fruit, reserving syrup and arrange in a shallow ovenproof serving dish. Spoon over a little of the syrup and cover with the cream mixture. Sprinkle over the sugar and pla dish under a preheated grill until the topping is bubbling and golden. Serve immediately.

Sauces
and
Relishes

BROILED APRICOTS

1lb/500g fresh apricots
2ozs/50g butter
4ozs/125g brown sugar

Wipe apricots, halve and remove stones. Place in a shallow pan, cut side up an. dot with butter. Sprinkle the sugar over the apricots and cook until the sugar melts. To be served with turkey, duck or pork.

Peaches may also be used for the above.

TANGY APRICOT SAUCE

8ozs/250g fresh apricots
1/4"/5mm slice of ginger
1tbsp/15ml lemon juice
1tbsp/15ml water

Halve the apricots. Remove the outer skin from the ginger and chop finely. P the ginger, apricots, lemon juice and water in a small saucepan, bring to the boil, cover and simmer slowly for about 15 minutes. Allow mixture to cool slightly and then skim off the stones. Pour the cooked fruit with liquid into a blender or food processor and purée. Deliciously sharp served with oily fish such as grilled mackerel.

DRIED APRICOT COULIS

-ozs/125g dried apricots
fl.ozs/250ml water
5ozs/45g caster sugar
sp/5ml arrowroot
tsp/10ml water
tbsp/60ml brandy

ut the apricots in a small saucepan and add the water and sugar. Bring to
he boil and simmer for about 6 minutes or until the apricots are soft and the
quid slightly reduced. Remove the apricots with a slotted spoon and reserve
e liquid in the saucepan. Mix the arrowroot with the two teaspoons of water
d add to the apricot liquid. Heat slowly, stirring continuously, until the liquid
ickens and clears. Put the apricots in a food processor or blender with the
uid and purée. Return the purée to the saucepan, add the brandy and heat,
t do not boil. Serve hot.

RICOT GLAZE

500g apricot jam
ce of half a lemon
sp/60ml water

pty jam into a small saucepan, add the lemon juice and water and bring
vly to the boil. Simmer for 5 minutes. If glaze is to be stored, strain
ugh a sieve and return to the heat, boiling for a futher 5 minutes before
ling and storing in a clean, warm jar and sealed.

sing immediately, continue boiling until the mixture thickens and brush
rously over the fruit.

APRICOT SAUCE

2tbsp/30ml apricot jam
5fl.ozs/150ml water
2 strips of lemon rind
1tbsp/15ml arrowroot
1tbsp/15ml water

Put the apricot jam, water and lemon rind in a saucepan and bring slowly to th
boil, stirring briskly. Adjust to taste by adding more jam or water as
necessary and if required thickened, add the arrowroot mixed with the water.
Heat until the sauce is to your liking and serve hot.

SPICED APRICOTS

7ozs/200g sugar
16fl.ozs/500ml boiling water
24 whole cloves
6 allspice berries
2"/5cm stick of cinnamon
Pinch of salt
1lb/500g apricots (halved and stones removed)

Put all the ingredients except for the apricots in a saucepan, bring to the bo
and simmer for about 15 minutes. Put the prepared apricots in a separate p
and cook until soft but not mushy. Drain fruit into a bowl and pour over the
spicy syrup. Leave to stand until it is cold, preferably overnight.

CHERRY RELISH

ozs/250g fresh cherries
tbsp/60ml water or juice from cherries
tbsp/45ml orange juice
bsp/15ml lemon juice
ozs/50g caster sugar

ook the cherries in a little water until soft and the stones can be removed
asily. Remove the cherries with a slotted spoon. Put cooked cherries in
nother saucepan with the water or juice from the cooked cherries, and add
he orange and lemon juices. Heat until warmed through and then put through
sieve or in a blender or food processor to purée. Return the purée to a small
n, add the sugar and heat slowly until it is dissolved. When the coulis is
eded, re-heat and serve with pancakes, souffles or ice creams.

HERRY PASTE

500g dark red cherries
jar

nove stalks and stones from the cherries, put them in a saucepan and cook
vly in a heavy-based pan for half an hour. Press the fruit through a sieve or
e in a food processor. Weigh the purée, add the equivalent amount of
ar and heat slowly. When the mixture forms a ball round the spoon, the
te is ready. Press into small pots and store in a cool place until needed.

CHERRY SAUCE (1)

1lb/500g red cherries
2ozs/50g granulated sugar
Pinch of cinnamon
5fl.ozs/150ml water
1tsp/5ml lemon juice (optional)
2tsp/10ml arrowroot
1tbsp/15ml water

Remove the stalks and stones from the cherries and put in a saucepan with the sugar and cinnamon. Cover pan and set on a low heat until the juice begins to run out of the fruit. Remove the cherries with a slotted spoon and add the wate to the juice. Simmer gently for about 5 minutes and then set aside. Check for sweetness at this stage. If too sweet, add a little lemon juice. Mix the arrowroo with 1 tablespoon/15ml water and add to the liquid. Bring to the boil and simme stirring continuously, until the mixture thickens. Reheat the cherries to put with the hot sauce and serve with a light sponge pudding.

CHERRY SAUCE (2)

6ozs/170g dark red cherries
8ozs/250g blackcurrant jelly
Small stick of cinnamon
12 cloves (tied in muslin)
10fl.ozs/300ml red wine

Remove stalks and stones from the cherries and put in a small saucepan with the blackcurrant jelly, cinnamon, cloves and red wine. Bring to the boil and sim gently for abot 10-15 minutes. Remove the cinnamon stick and cloves and ser sauce with venison or roast duck.

SPICED PEACHES

lb/500g fresh ripe peaches
7ozs/200g granulated sugar
6fl.ozs/500ml boiling water
24 whole cloves and 6 allspice berries (tied in a muslin bag)
2"/5cm cinnamon stick
A pinch of salt

Remove the skins from the peaches. If you pour boiling water over them the skins will split and remove easily. Halve the fruit and remove the stones. Poach each halves gently in a little water until they are soft and then remove with a slotted spoon onto a serving dish.

Put the sugar, water, spices and salt in a saucepan, bring to the boil slowly while the sugar dissolves and simmer slowly for about 10-15 minutes. Remove the muslin bag and the cinnamon stick. Pour the syrup over the cooked peaches.

Tinned peaches may be used for this recipe.

TEA PLUM COMPOTE

500g fresh ripe plums
fl.ozs/500ml black tea (sweetened)
zs/125g granulated sugar
tbsp/30ml rum

Take the plums, halve and remove stones. Place in a basin and pour over the warm tea. Leave to stand for 24 hours. Remove the plums with a slotted spoon onto a serving dish and put the liquid in a small saucepan. Add the sugar to the liquid (adjusting to taste) and heat to allow it to dissolve. Add the rum, bring to boiling point and pour over the fruit immediately. Leave to stand for about 2 hours before serving.

PLUM SAUCE

PLUM SAUCE

2lbs/1kg plums
8ozs/250g granulated sugar
1pt/600ml vinegar
1 teaspoon of salt
1 teaspoon ground ginger
1/2 tsp cayenne pepper
1/4 tsp ground cloves

Wipe plums, halve and remove stones. Chop the fruit, put the stones in a muslin bag and place in a saucepan with a little water. Bring to the boil and simmer over a low heat for about 10 minutes. Add all the other ingredients, m well and bring to the boil. Simmer gently for half an hour. Remove the muslin bag with the stones and discard. Press the mixture through a sieve or puree i a blender or food processor and return the juice to a saucepan. Cook over a gentle heat for another 30 minutes, stirring occasionally.

Pour liquid into clean warmed jars, wipe rims and cover, but with the lids slight loosened. Place jars in a large pan and pour boiling water round them. Heat water slowly and simmer gently for 30 minutes to sterilise. Remove the bottles carefully and tighten lids immediately. Store in a cool dark place.

PLUM CATSUP

PLUM CATSUP

2.5lbs/1.25kg plums
1 large cooking apple
8fl.ozs/250ml vinegar
10ozs/285g brown sugar
1/2 oz/13g powdered cinnamon
1tsp/5ml powdered cloves
1tsp/5ml salt
Pinch of mace

Halve the plums and remove the stones. Cut the apple into quarters but do not peel or core. Place fruit in a large saucepan with the vinegar and cook u it is tender. Put cooked fruit in a blender or food processor to purée. Put t purée in a saucepan and add the sugar, cinnamon, cloves, salt and mace. B to the boil and simmer until the mixture thickens. Put into clean warm jars, wipe rims and cover.

102

PRUNE SAUCE

8ozs/250g stoned prunes
2tbsp/30ml lemon juice
1tbsp/15ml finely grated lemon rind
3 whole cloves
Pinch of cinnamon
Pinch of ground allspice
Half teaspoon grated nutmeg
8fl.ozs/250ml water
4ozs/125g granulated sugar
4fl.ozs/125ml red wine vinegar

Put the prunes, lemon juice and rind, cloves, cinnamon, allspice and nutmeg in a heavy-based saucepan. Add sufficient water just to cover and bring to the boil. Simmer for about 15 minutes or until the prunes are soft and the liquid reduced to about half. Remove the cloves and puree the cooked prunes in a blender or food processor. Return purée to the saucepan, add the sugar and vinegar and cook over a low heat, stirring continuously until the sauce is smooth and warmed through. Serve with roast pork.

Preserves
and
Jams

A few tips which may help when making jam or preserves.

1. Before using, all containers should be washed in hot, soapy water and rinsed thoroughly in hot water. Dry containers in a warm oven and handle them as little as possible.

2. There are two ways to test for setting point -

a) by using a sugar thermometer which should be dipped in hot water before being used to test the jam. Submerge the thermometer bulb completely and setting point is reached when the thermometer registers 105C/221F.

b) by using a cold plate. Pour a small amount of the jam on a cold plate and leave to stand until it is cold. Run your finger across the top and if the surface wrinkles, it is ready. If it is not ready return to the heat for about five minutes before repeating the test. When ready, remove jam from the heat immediately.

3. Wipe the rim of the containers with a damp cloth before placing a waxed disc on the top of the contents and then covering with a top or cellophane secured with a rubber band.

4. Always store preserves and jams in a cool, dark place.

APRICOT & ALMOND PRESERVE

1lb/500g dried apricots
2pts/1.13lt water
2lbs8ozs/1.25kg preserving sugar
½ tsp/3ml almond essence
2ozs/50g flaked almonds

Put the apricots in a bowl and pour over the water. Leave to soak overnight. Drain off the liquid into a heavy-based saucepan and add the sugar. Bring to the boil slowly, stirring while the sugar dissolves, add the apricots and bring the boil. Check for setting by using a jam thermometer or the cold plate method. Stir in the almond essence and flaked almonds and remove from he Leave to stand for 10 minutes, stirring occasionally to keep the fruit and almonds well distributed. Pour into clean warm jars and seal tightly. Store in a cool dark place.

APRICOT CURD

8ozs/250g fresh apricots
A little water
8ozs/250g caster sugar
Juice and grated rind of 1 lemon
2ozs/50g butter
2 eggs (beaten)

Wash the apricots, halve and remove the stones. Put in a saucepan with a
little water and cook until soft. Put cooked fruit with any liquid through a sieve
or in a blender or food processor to purée. Transfer purée to a double
saucepan and add the sugar, butter and juice and grated lemon rind. When the
sugar has dissolved, add the beaten eggs and stir the mixture until it thickens.
Pour into clean warmed jars and cover.

APRICOT JAM

4lbs/2kgs fresh ripe apricots
15fl.ozs/425ml water
4lbs/2kg preserving sugar
Juice of 1 lemon

Cut the apricots in half, remove the stones and put in a large pan with the
water. Add the lemon juice. Crack a few of the stones and remove the kernals
and add to the pan. Bring to the boil and simmer until the apricots are soft.
Add the sugar, heat gently while it dissolves, and stir frequently. Boil rapidly
for about 15 minutes or until setting point is reached. Remove from the heat
and leave to stand for about 10 minutes in the pan. Pour into clean warm jars,
cover and seal. Should make about 6lbs/3kgs of jam.

APRICOT & RASPBERRY JAM

2lbs/1kg fresh ripe apricots
Half pint/300ml water
1lb/500g raspberries
3lbs/1.5kg preserving sugar
1oz/25g butter

Halve the apricots, remove the stones and put in a large heavy-based pan.
Crack a few of the stones, remove the kernals and add to prepared apricots.
Add the water and bring to the boil and simmer for about 10 minutes or until
the fruit is soft. Add the raspberries and mix well. Gradually add the sugar,
heating slowly and stirring while it dissolves. Bring to the boil and boil hard
until setting point is reached. Add the butter to disperse the scum and pour
jam into clean, warm jars. Wipe jars and cover. Should make about 5lbs/2.25k

APRICOT PASTE

4lb/2kgs fresh apricots
1pt/600ml water
4lbs/2kgs sugar

Half the fruit, remove the stones and put in a saucepan with the water. Cook
the fruit until it is soft and then press through a sieve or purée in a food
processor or blender. Weigh the purée and add the same weight in sugar.
Return the purée and sugar to a slow heat and cook until the mixture is thic
and does not stick to the pan. Press paste into flat moulds and leave in a v
cool oven (110C/225F/Gas Mark 1/4) for about six hours. Remove from the
moulds and sprinkle generously with caster sugar. Store in airtight tins.

PRESERVED APRICOTS IN SYRUP

lbs/2.5kgs good ripe apricots
b8ozs/675g granulated sugar
Ofl.ozs/850ml water

nmerse the apricots in boiling water, remove the stones and place in
reserving jars. Do not bruise the fruit but pack in tightly. Put the sugar and
ater in a pan, heat slowly while the sugar dissolves and boil for 1 minute.
ur over the fruit in the jars ensuring the fruit is covered. Put the lids on the
rs but do not screw down. Place jars in a large pan and pour boiling water
und them. Keep the water boiling gently for 25 minutes to sterilise.
move jars and screw lids down tightly. Store in a cool dark place.

APRICOT CHUTNEY

zs/250g dried apricots
/600ml white vinegar
s/125g raisins (chopped)
s/125g sultanas
p/15ml pickling spice (in a muslin bag)
/5ml salt
arlic cloves (crushed)
non - finely peeled and juice extracted
500g prepared cooking apples (peeled, cored and chopped)
500g brown sugar

the apricots into small pieces and soak for about 3 hours in cold water.
n and put in a saucepan with 2tbsp/30ml of the vinegar. Add the chopped
ns, sultanas, pickling spice, salt, crushed garlic and juice and lemon rind.
g mixture to the boil and simmer for 30 minutes, gradually adding the
aining vinegar. Add the apples and sugar, stir until sugar is dissolved and
for a further 20 minutes or until mixture thickens. Remove the muslin bag
ckling spices, put chutney into clean warm jars and cover.

PEACHES IN BRANDY

6 firm ripe peaches
24fl.ozs/750ml water
12ozs/350g granulated sugar
Brandy

Remove the skins from the peaches by dipping fruit briefly in hot water to make
the skins split and remove easily. Prick each peach twice with a fork. Put the
water and sugar in a saucepan, bring to the boil slowly while the sugar
dissolves, stirring occasionally, and then boil for 10 minutes to make the syrup.
Poach the peaches a few at a time for about 5 minutes until they are tender
but still firm. Pack into clean warm jars and add 2 tablespoons/30ml of brandy
to each jar, topping up with the syrup. Seal and store for at least a month
before using.

Apricots and cherries (with stalks removed) can be used for this recipe.
Use firm fruits and adjust the water and sugar accordingly.

CHERRY OLIVES

2lbs/1kg Morello cherries
Salt
Vinegar

Wash the cherries but do not remove stalks or stones. Pack into jars and to
each jar add 1½ teaspoons/8ml salt, 4fl.ozs/125ml vinegar and top up with c
water. Seal and turn jars upside down and leave for two weeks before using.

SWEET CHERRY OLIVES

2lbs/1kg large white cherries
Sugar
Vinegar

Wash the cherries but do not remove stalks or stones. Pack into jars and to each jar add 1½ teaspoons/8ml sugar, 4fl.ozs/125ml vinegar and top up with cold water. Seal and turn jars upside down and leave for two weeks before using.

PICKLED CHERRIES

2lbs/1kg firm sour cherries
Vinegar
Sugar

Remove stalks and stones from cherries. Place in a bowl and cover with vinegar. Drain the cherries and weigh them. Put in a stone jar and add an equal amount sugar. Cover and stir once a day until the sugar is completely dissolved - about 7 days.

QUICK RASPBERRY JAM

1lb/500g raspberries
2tbsp/30ml lemon juice
1lb/500g sugar

Remove the stalks from the raspberries and put in a large microwave safe bowl.
Add the sugar and lemon juice and stir lightly. Microwave on full power for 5
minutes, stirring occasionally until sugar dissolves. Microwave again on full
power for 12 minutes or until jam reaches setting point or 221F/105C. Leave t
stand for at least 5 minutes. Stir well and then ladle into clean, warm jars.
Wipe jars with a damp cloth and cover.

RASPBERRY JELLY

4lbs/1.75kg raspberries
Sugar
1pt/600ml water

Wash the fruit, put in a pan with the water and simmer until soft. Place in a
jelly bag and leave to drain overnight. Measure the juice and allow 1lb/500g
sugar to 1pt/600ml of juice. Put the juice and sugar in a pan and heat slow
stirring continuously, while the sugar dissolves. Bring to the boil and cook
rapidly until setting point is reached. Pour into clean, warm jars, wipe clean
with a damp cloth, cover and seal.

CHERRY JAM

4lbs/2kgs cherries (weight after stalks and stones removed)
8fl.ozs/250ml water
4lbs/2kgs preserving sugar

Put the stoned cherries in a heavy-based pan with the water and bring to the boil. When boiling, pour through a sieve and put the juice in another saucepan. Add the sugar to the juice and boil for 10 minutes. Add the cherries to the syrup and boil again for one minute. Remove from the heat and leave to stand for two minutes; return to the heat and bring to the boil again. Repeat once more. Pour into clean warmed jars and seal.

SUNSHINE CHERRIES

2lbs/1kg unblemished Morello cherries
2lbs/1kg sugar

Wash cherries and arrange in layers with the sugar in a deep pan. Leave to stand for about half an hour, then bring to the boil and cook until they are tender but still firm. Spread the cherries on a platter, cover with glass and set in the sun for a few days or until the syrup is thick. Stir gently several times each day and bring indoors after sunset.
Serve with ice cream.

RASPBERRY SYRUP

1lb/500g raspberries
1lb/500g redcurrants
2lbs/1kg sugar

Use ripe fruit and crush through a fine sieve. Put the juice and sugar in a saucepan and bring to the boil. Allow it to boil for five minutes and remove from heat. Skim the juice, pour into a jug and allow to cool before bottling and covering.

PRESERVED RASPBERRIES

6lbs/3kgs raspberries
2lbs/1kg sugar
2pts/1200ml water

Put the fruit in a large bowl. Put the sugar and water in a large saucepan, he. gradually while the sugar dissolves and then boil for about three minutes. Pou the boiling syrup over the fruit and leave to stand for 15 minutes. Take the fr out carefully with a draining spoon and place in clean jars. Return the juice t the heat and boil for another 15 minutes. Pour it over the fruit, wipe the edge of the jars and put the lids on. Place the jars in a pan with boiling water for about 20 minutes and then remove and leave to cool.

CHERRY & APPLE JAM

2lbs/1kg cherries
2lbs/1kg cooking apples
Juice of 2 lemons
2pts/1.1l water
2lbs8ozs/1.25kg sugar
/2 oz/13g butter

Remove stones from the cherries and put in a large saucepan. Peel, core and thickly slice the apples, sprinkle the lemon juice over them to prevent from browning. Set aside. Put the apple peel and cores in the saucepan with the cherry stones and add the water. Bring to the boil and cook uncovered until the liquid is reduced by about one-third. This will take about 45-60 minutes. Press the cooked pulp through a sieve and return to a clean pan. Add the prepared fruit and bring the mixture slowly to the boil. Cover the pan and simmer slowly, stirring occasionally, for about 15 minutes or until the fruit is tender. Gradually add the sugar, heating gently and stirring continuously, until all the sugar is dissolved. Then bring the jam to a fast boil and cook until setting point is reached. Stir in the butter which will disperse any scum. Pour into clean warmed jars and seal.

DAMSON PICKLE

bs/2kg damsons
bs/1.5kg demerara sugar
fl.ozs/300ml vinegar
oz/8g cinnamon
oz/8g cloves (tied in a muslin bag)

Put the sugar, spices and vinegar in a saucepan and cook for 10 minutes. Remove the cloves and add the damsons. Bring to the boil and simmer gently for a further 10 minutes, ensuring the fruit remains whole. Put all the mixture into a large jar and seal when cold. Serve with cold meat.

Plums may also be used for this recipe.

DAMSON JAM

4lbs/2kg ripe damsons
4lbs/2kg preserving sugar
5fl.ozs/150ml vinegar
5fl.ozs/150ml water

Put the sugar, vinegar and water in a pan. Bring to the boil slowly while the sugar dissolves and then cook rapidly until the liquid becomes syrupy. Add the fruit and cook for 10 minutes when setting point should be reached. Boil a little longer if necessary and check again for setting. Pour into clean warm jars and seal.

GREENGAGE JAM

5lbs/2.5kg ripe greengages
4tbsp/60ml water
Preserving sugar

Remove the stones from the greengages and weigh. Allow the equivalent in weight of preserving sugar. Put the greengages in pan with the water, bring to the boil and cook until fruit is soft. Add the sugar and continue stirring until is dissolved. Bring rapidly to the boil and cook until setting point is reached. Pour into clean warm jars and seal.

Plums may also be used for this recipe.

PRESERVED GREENGAGES IN SYRUP

5lbs/2.5kgs good firm greengages
1lb8ozs/675kg sugar
30fl.ozs/860ml water

Wash the fruit, dry thoroughly and remove any stalks. Put the sugar and water
n a pan, bring to the boil and cook until it becomes syrupy. Place the fruit in
clean preserving jars and pour the boiling syrup over them. Stand the jars, with
the lids loosened, in a large pan and surrounded with boiling water. Simmer for
0 minutes and then remove the jars. Tighten the lids and store in a cool dark
place.

Plums may also be preserved in this way.

CKLED PEACHES

fresh firm peaches
l.ozs/250ml vinegar
l.ozs/250ml water
zs/150g brown sugar
zs/200g white sugar
/25g cloves
innamon stick broken into pieces

 the peaches quickly in boiling water to remove the skins easily, then halve
d remove the stones. Put the cloves and broken cinnamon stick into a muslin
. Place the vinegar, water, sugars and spices in a saucepan, bring to the
 slowly while the sugar dissolves and simmer for 5 minutes. Poach the fruit
he syrup a few at a time until it is tender and remove with a slotted spoon.
k fruit into clean warm jars and add the syrup to within 1/4"/5mm of the top
he jars. Seal and store in a cool, dark place.

PEACH CONSERVE

4lbs/2kg firm peaches
10fl.ozs/300ml water
Juice of 2 lemons (strained)
2lbs/1kg preserving sugar

Remove the skins and stones from the peaches and chop the flesh. Put in a large heavy-based pan with the water and lemon juice, bring to the boil and simmer until the peaches are very soft. Gradually add the sugar, heating gently and stirring continuously, until the sugar has been dissolved. Bring to a fast boil and keep at a rolling boil until setting point is reached. Remove from heat and stand for 5 minutes, stirring occasionally. Pour into clean warm jars and cover.

NATURAL PRESERVED PEACHES

5lb/2.5kg good peaches

Remove skins from peaches by dipping fruit in hot water and then halve and take out stones. Place fruit well packed in clean preserving jars with lids loosened. Stand the jars in boiling water and simmer for 25 minutes to sterilise. Remove and tighten lids. Fruit will be ideal for use in pies or tarts or with milk pudding

PEACH CHUTNEY

2lbs/1kg peaches
1lb/500g chopped onions
10fl.ozs/300ml red wine vinegar
3ozs/75g chopped dates
3ozs/75g raisins
1tsp/5ml salt
½ tsp ground ginger
½ tsp ground cinnamon
¼ tsp ground cloves
1tbsp/15ml mustard seeds
Grated peel and juice of 1 lemon
8ozs/250g brown sugar

Peel, stone and chop the peaches and put in a saucepan with all the
ingredients, except for the sugar. Bring to the boil, stirring from time to time,
and then leave to simmer until the peaches and onions are tender. Add the
sugar and stir until it is dissolved. Simmer chutney gently for 2-3 hours or
until it is a rich brown in colour and thick, stirring frequently to prevent it
sticking to the pan. Pour into clean warm jars and seal. Store in a cool dark
place and start to use after about 6 weeks.

DRIED PEACHES

5s/2.5kgs firm ripe peaches

Set oven 110C/225F/Gas Mark ¼ or better still the coolest part of an Aga or
similar.

prepare the peaches, cut them in half, remove the stones and cut the flesh
to quarters. Arrange cut side up on thick paper on a baking tray and put in a
warm oven until they are dry.

Apricots and plums may also be dried. Ensure that the fruit is unblemished
the plums should be wiped.

ALMOND GATEAU WITH RASPBERRIES

4 eggs (separated)
7ozs/200g caster sugar
3½ ozs/100g ground almonds
Grated rind and juice of half a lemon
3½ ozs/100g semolina

For the icing -
2ozs/50g granulated sugar
5fl.ozs/150ml water
8ozs/250g icing sugar
Lemon flavouring

1lb/500g raspberries
Caster sugar (to taste)
Set oven at 375F/190C/Gas Mark 5.

Grease and line a 9"/23cm deep cake tin. Beat the egg yolks and sugar
together until thick and creamy. Gradually work in the ground almonds and
lemon rind and juice and then leave to stand for a few minutes. Whisk the egg
whites until stiff and fold into the almond mixture with the semolina. Turn the
mixture into the prepared cake tin and bake for about 50 minutes. Leave to
cool.

To make the icing, dissolve the granulated sugar in the water, bring to the boil
and boil steadily for 10 minutes. Remove the pan from the heat and leave to
get quite cold. Add the icing sugar, a little at a time and beating well with a
wooden spoon. Add the lemon flavouring. The icing should coat the back of the
spoon and look glossy. Warm the pan on a very low heat, do not allow it to get
too hot.

Place the cake on a serving dish and pour over the glace icing. Serve with the
raspberries in a separate dish and sprinkled with caster sugar.

LUXURY PLUM JAM

3lbs/1.5kg plums
5fl.ozs/150ml water
8tbsp/120ml lemon juice
3lbs8ozs/1.5kg preserving sugar
4tbsp/60ml cherry brandy
½ oz/13g butter

Remove stones from the plums and chop the flesh. Put the plums and water in a large pan and cook over a low heat until the fruit is soft. Stir in the lemon juice and simmer for a further 5 minutes. Add the sugar and keep stirring while it dissolves. Increase the heat and boil jam rapidly until setting point is reached. Remove from the heat and stir in the cherry brandy. Add the butter to disperse the scum and leave for 5 minutes. Stir well and ladle into clean warm jars. Cover and store in a cool dark place.

PLUM & APPLE JAM

3lbs/1.5kg apples
3lbs/1.5kg plums (washed)
/600ml water
6lbs/3kgs preserving sugar
Juice of 2 lemons
1tsp/5ml cinnamon

Peel, core and slice the apples and put the peel and cores in a muslin bag. Put the sliced apple, plums and muslin bag in a large pan, add the water and cook until the fruit in reduced to a pulp, stirring from time to time. Remove the muslin bag containing the peel and cores. Add the sugar, lemon juice and cinnamon and stir well until the sugar is dissolved. Bring to the boil and cook until setting point is reached. Pour into clean warm jars and seal.

PLUM, RAISIN AND RUM CONSERVE

4lbs/2kg plums
6ozs/175g raisins
10fl.ozs/300ml water
1lb8ozs/1.2kg preserving sugar
4tbsp/60ml dark rum

Wash the plums, halve and remove stones. Place the plums and raisins in a large saucepan, with the stones in a muslin bag, and half the water. Bring to the boil and simmer until the plums are soft. If they are not very juicy, add more of the water. Add the sugar and keep stirring while it dissolves. Increase the heat and boil rapidly until mixture is thickened. Remove from the heat and stir in the rum. Pour into clean warm jars and cover.

PLUM CHUTNEY

2lb/1kg plums
4ozs/125g mixed sultanas and raisins
1tbsp/15ml pickling spices (tied in a muslin bag)
1 teaspoon salt
1 teaspoon ground ginger
10fl.ozs/300ml vinegar
12ozs/350g brown sugar

Wash the plums, halve and remove stones. Put the plums, dried fruit, spices, salt and ginger in a saucepan and just cover with some of the vinegar. Simmer gently until the fruit is soft, stirring occasionally. Add the rest of the vinegar and stir in the sugar, heating slowly while it dissolves. Bring to the boil and simmer steadily until the mixture thickens. Remove the muslin bag, pour the chutney into clean warm jars and seal.

PLUM AND ORANGE CONSERVE

lbs/1.5kg plums
b/500g seedless raisins
 oranges
lbs/1.5kg granulated sugar

ipe the plums, remove stones and cut into quarters. Chop the raisins. Wipe
ie oranges, cut into thin slices and remove pips. Put all the fruit in a large
eavy based pan and add the sugar. Bring mixture to the boil slowly, stirring
onstantly, while the sugar dissolves and then leave to simmer until the
ixture thickens. Ladle into clean warm jars and seal.

UNES IN BRANDY

500g stoned prunes
zs/125g sugar
ozs/250ml water
ınamon stick
d of 1 lemon cut into strips
ozs/250ml brandy

the prunes, sugar, water, cinnamon and lemon peel in a saucepan and poach
5 minutes. Remove the prunes with a slotted spoon and pack into a clean
n jar. Return the liquid to the heat and boil until you are left with about
ozs/90ml. Remove the peel and cinnamon and leave to cool. Half fill the jar
brandy and top up with the syrup. Add a little more brandy to cover
es if necessary. Seal jar and store in a cool dark place for 3 weeks before
g.

SPICY PRUNES

1lb/500g large stoned prunes
16fl.ozs/500ml cold black tea
1pt/600ml white wine vinegar
1lb/500g sugar
1 cinnamon stick
1tsp/5ml cloves
10 allspice berries
Blade of mace

Put the prunes in a large bowl and cover with the cold tea. Leave to stand for 12 hours. Tip the prunes and liquid into a large saucepan and cook over a low heat for about 15-20 minutes until the prunes are plump. Put the vinegar, sugar and spices in another saucepan, bring to the boil slowly while the sugar dissolves and then simmer for 5 minutes. Add the prunes and the liquid and simmer for a further 5 minutes. Using a slotted spoon remove the prunes and pack into warm clean jars. Turn up the heat to bring the syrup back to the boil, remove the spices, and then ladle over the prunes ensuring they are covered. Seal and leave for a week before using.

SLOE AND APPLE JELLY

Equal quantities of sloe berries and apples
Water
Sugar

Chop the apples and put in a pan with the sloes. Add sufficient water just to cover the fruit and cook until it is really soft. Strain cooked mixture through jelly bag or several layers of muslin and weigh the juice. Allow 1lb/500g sugar each 1pint/600ml of juice. Put juice and sugar in a saucepan, heat slowly, stirring frequently, until sugar is dissolved and then boil until setting point is reached. Spoon into clean warm jars and seal. Can be used with roast lamb, pork or rabbit.

Cakes
and
Gateaux

APRICOT GATEAU

2lbs/1kg fresh apricots
1lb8ozs/675g caster sugar
8fl.ozs/250ml water
2 eggs
4ozs/125g self-raising flour
4ozs/125g butter (melted)

Halve and stone the apricots, put in a pan with the 1lb4ozs/525g of the sugar and water and bring to the boil slowly while the sugar dissolves. Cook until the fruit becomes transparent and then leave to slightly cool before putting in a blender or food processor to make a purée.

Set oven at 150C/300F/Gas Mark 2.

Put the remaining sugar in a bowl with the eggs and beat until light and crear Add the melted butter and flour, stirring until the mixture is smooth. Pour in a well buttered baking tin and cook for about 40 minutes until light and well risen. Remove carefully from the tin and leave on a wire rack to cool. When ready to serve, put on a serving dish and spread the apricot purée over the t Sprinkle over a little caster sugar and serve with whipped fresh cream.

CRUNCHY APRICOT CAKE

ozs/250g fresh apricots
fl.ozs/190ml water
ozs/50g granulated sugar
ozs/175g digestive biscuits
ozs/50g butter or margarine
/500g curd cheese
ozs/125g caster sugar
arge egg (well beaten)
few drops of vanilla essence
esh whipped cream

t oven at 180C/350F/Gas Mark 4.

pe the apricots, halve and remove stones. Put the water and granulated
gar in a saucepan and bring to the boil slowly while the sugar dissolves. Boil
a few minutes until the liquid becomes syrupy and then poach the apricots
the syrup until they are tender but not pulpy. Crush the biscuits with a
ling pin and lightly grease a flan tin.

the curd cheese through a strainer into a bowl and gradually beat in the
ter or margarine and the sugar, followed by the egg. Beat the mixture until
light and fluffy. Blend in the vanilla essence. Sprinkle half the biscuit
mbs over the bottom and sides of the tin and then spoon in the curd
ture. Smooth the top and sprinkle over the remainder of the crumbs. Bake
about 30 minutes. Take out from the oven and leave in the tin for at least
hours before removing and placing carefully on a serving dish. Drain the
cots and arrange over the top of the cake. Put the syrup in a small
cepan and boil until it thickens. Spoon over the apricots and serve with the
ped cream.

CHERRY CAKES

4ozs/125g soft margarine
4ozs/125g caster sugar
2 eggs
4ozs/125g self-raising flour
1tsp/5ml baking powder
5fl.ozs/150ml whipped double cream
4ozs/125g dark red cherries

Set oven at 200C/400F/Gas Mark 6.

Put the margarine, sugar, eggs, flour and baking powder in a bowl and beat well together with a wooden spoon until the mixture is really smooth. Divide the mixture between 12-16 cake cases on a baking tray and cook for about 15-20 minutes. Leave to cool on a wire rack. Wipe the cherries and carefully remove the stalks and stones. Put a little whipped cream on each cake and top with a cherry. Serve immediately.

APRICOT KUCHEN

12ozs/350g fresh ripe apricots
2 eggs
A few drops of vanilla essence
6ozs/175g caster sugar
4ozs/125g self-raising flour
1/2 tsp baking powder
Pinch of salt
4fl.ozs/125ml milk
1oz/25g butter
4ozs/125g demerara sugar
1/2 tsp cinnamon powder
Set oven at 180C/350F/Gas Mark 4.

Wipe the apricots, halve and remove stones. Put the eggs and essence in a bowl and beat until thick. Gradually add the caster sugar with the flour, baking powder and salt and beat until smooth. Put the milk in a saucepan with the butter and heat gently until the butter is melted. Stir into the first mixture and beat until all ingredients are well blended. Pour mixture into a well buttered baking dish and press the halved apricots into the mixture, cut side up.
Mix the cinnamon into the demerara sugar and sprinkle over the fruit.
Bake for about 25-30 minutes when it should be golden brown and well risen.
Can be served hot or cold.

PEACH MUFFINS

10ozs/285g self raising flour
1tsp/15ml baking powder
pinch of salt
4ozs/125g caster sugar
2 eggs (lightly beaten)
9 fl.ozs/250ml milk
1oz/25g melted butter
4ozs/125g chopped tinned or fresh peaches

Set oven at 200C/400F/Gas Mark 6.

Sift the flour, baking powder and salt into a bowl and mix in the sugar. In another bowl mix the eggs, milk, melted butter and chopped peaches. Pour this mixture into the flour and stir in lightly. Spoon mixture into buttered muffin tins or large cake cases, about two-thirds full, and bake for about 15-20 minutes until light golden brown and well risen.

PEACH AND NUT DELIGHT

For the nutty layers -
5 egg whites
7ozs/200g caster sugar
2ozs/50g hazelnuts ground and toasted
3ozs/75g ground walnuts
3ozs/75g plain flour (sifted)
2ozs/50g butter

4-5 fresh ripe peaches
2ozs/50g plain chocolate (grated)
10fl.ozs/300ml double cream
1 teaspoon caster sugar
A few drops of vanilla essence
2ozs/50g sifted icing sugar

Set oven at 180C/350F/Gas Mark 4.

Using baking paper, mark four circles 8"/20cm in diameter and place on a
baking sheet. Whisk the egg whites until stiff and dry and lightly fold in the
caster sugar, sifted flour and nuts. Soften the butter but do not let it becor
oily and fold into the egg mixture. Divide the mixture evenly and spread in eac
of the four circles. Bake for about 30 minutes or until the layers are a light
golden brown. Remove carefully from baking sheet and leave to cool on a wire
rack.

Scald the peaches to remove the skins, halve and remove stones, and chop th
flesh. Whip the cream until really firm and add the caster sugar and vanilla
essence, beating in thoroughly. Then stir in the chopped peaches.

Just before serving, prepare the delight in layers, starting and finishing with
nutty layer and reserving a little of the cream for the sides. Sprinkle the
grated chocolate over the sides and sprinkle the top generously with the icin
sugar. Serve immediately.

ALMOND CAKE WITH PLUMS

For the cake -
4ozs/125g butter
5ozs/150g caster sugar
3 eggs
3ozs/75g ground almonds
2ozs/50g plain flour
A few drops of almond essence

1lb/500g red plums
3tbsp/45ml red wine or port
4tbsp/60ml redcurrant jelly
Grated rind and juice of 1 orange

Put the butter in a bowl and beat with a wooden spoon. Gradually add the
sugar and continue beating until the mixture is soft and smooth. Add the
eggs, one at a time with one-third of the ground almonds, beating continuously,
until the last egg and ground almonds have been added and blended thoroughly.
Then lightly fold in the flour and almond essence. Turn mixture into a well
buttered deep cake tin base lined with a round of baking paper and bake for
about 45 minutes when the cake should be golden brown. Test to see if it is
cooked by inserting a skewer which should come out clean. Remove from the tin
carefully and peel away the paper base. Leave on a cake rack to cool completely
and dust the top with a little caster sugar.

While the cake is cooking prepare the plums. Wipe the plums, halve and remove
stones. Put the wine in a pan (large enough to take the plums) and boil until
the quantity is reduced to about half. Add the redcurrant jelly and stir until it
is dissolved and then mix in the orange rind and juice. Put the plums, cut side
down in the pan and let the syrup lightly poach the fruit until it is quite tender.
Turn into a glass bowl and leave to cool. Serve with the almond cake.

PRUNE BREAD

8ozs/250g caster sugar
2ozs/50g melted butter
1 egg (well beaten)
6ozs/175g chopped prunes
4fl.ozs/125ml prune juice
8fl.ozs/250ml sour milk*
4ozs/125g wholemeal flour
8ozs/250g self-raising flour
1 teaspoon bicarbonate of soda
1/4 tsp baking powder
Pinch of salt

Set oven at 180C/350F/Gas Mark 4.

Put the sugar, butter and egg in a bowl and beat together until creamy. Add the chopped prunes, prune juice and sour milk and mix well. In a separate bowl sift together all the dry ingredients and add to the creamed mixture. Mix thoroughly and turn into 1x2lb/1kg or 2x1lb/500g loaf tins which have been well greased. Bake for about an hour and when cooked remove from tin and leave t cool on a wire rack.

* Milk may be soured by adding 1 tablespoon/15ml of lemon juice or vinegar to every 10fl.ozs/300ml of milk.

PRUNE GINGERBREAD

8ozs/250g plain flour
.1/2 tsp bicarbonate of soda
.1/2 tsp ground ginger
Pinch of salt
12ozs/350g black treacle
3ozs/75g butter or margarine
4fl.ozs/125ml sour milk (see recipe for Prune Bread on page 132)
1 egg

Set oven at 160C/325F/Gas Mark 3.

Sift all the dry ingredients into a bowl. Put the treacle and butter or margarine in a small saucepan and put on a gentle heat to blend well, stirring frequently. Set aside to cool. When the treacle is quite cool add the sour milk and beaten egg, stir well to blend in thoroughly. Pour into the dry ingredients and mix to a smooth batter. Spoon mixture into a well greased and base lined deep baking tin about 8"/20cm or 9"/30cm square and bake for about 35 minutes. Remove carefully from tin and leave to cool.

PRUNE COOKIES

Half a tin of condensed milk
4ozs/125g shredded coconut
Pinch of salt
6ozs/175g prunes (finely chopped)
8ozs/250g cornflakes
Few drops of vanilla essence

Set oven at 180C/350F/Gas Mark 4.

Mix all the ingredients thoroughly together. Shape into small balls and place on a baking sheet lined with baking paper. Cook for 10 minutes.

PRUNE OATMEAL BREAD

16fl.ozs/500ml boiling water
3ozs/75g rolled oats
6ozs/175g black treacle
1 teaspoon salt
1oz/25g butter
4fl.ozs/125ml lukewarm water
1 pack of yeast
1lb/500g plain flour

Put the rolled oats into a bowl and pour over the boiling water. Stir thoroughly and leave to stand for an hour. Then add the treacle, salt and butter and mix well. Put the lukewarm water and yeast in a small bowl and when it has dissolved, add to the oatmeal. Stir in the flour and beat thoroughly. Cover bowl and leave in a warm place to double in quantity. Knead the dough on a floured board and add more flour to the dough if a little sticky. Shape into loaves and place in buttered pans. Leave to rise again until almost double.

Set oven at 180C/350F/Gas Mark 4.

Bake for about 45-50 minutes. Leave on a wire rack to cool.

PRUNE CAKE

7ozs/200g dried stoned prunes
5fl.ozs/150ml boiling water
Grated zest of 1 lemon
5fl.ozs/150ml red wine

6ozs/175g butter or margarine
7ozs/200g caster sugar
7ozs/200g plain flour
3 large eggs (beaten)
1 teaspoon baking powder
1oz/25g melted butter

Prepare the prunes first. Put the prunes in a bowl, pour over the boiling water and leave to soak for an hour. Remove prunes and cut them in half. Put them into a saucepan with the liquid, add the lemon zest and red wine and cook with the lid off until all the liquid has evaporated. Leave to cool.

Set oven at 180C/350F/Gas Mark 4.

Put the butter or margarine in a bowl with the sugar and beat until smooth. Sift the flour and baking powder together and gradually add to the creamed mixture with the eggs. Beat mixture until it is really smooth. Well grease and line a 9"/23cm cake tin and spoon the mixture into it. Arrange the prunes evenly on the top and bake for 50-60 minutes until it is golden brown and well risen. This can be used warm as a pudding served with custard or cream or eaten cold as a cake.

PRUNE GATEAU

1lb/500g good quality stoned prunes
8ozs/250g plain flour
4ozs/125g butter
2 eggs (separated)

For the cream -
10ozs/285g plain flour
10fl.ozs/300ml boiling milk
4ozs/125g caster sugar
2 eggs
2ozs/50g butter (cut into small pieces)
A few drops of vanilla essence

Stand the prunes in some lukewarm water for half an hour and then drain.

Put the 8ozs/250g plain flour in a basin, add the 4ozs/125g butter and egg yolks and beat until smooth. Whisk the egg whites until firm and work into the paste. Roll out the paste on a lightly floured board and spread it on the base of a well greased baking tin. Arrange the prunes on the paste.

To make the cream, put the sugar and eggs in a pan and mix well together. Ac the flour, blend until smooth and slowly pour in the boiling milk with the vanilla essence - stirring continuously. Bring mixture to the boil and cook for 1 minut still stirring. Stir in the butter and blend well. Pour over the prunes and leav to set. Serve cold.

Confectionery

FRUITY CHEWS

3ozs/85g dried apricots
3ozs/85g stoned prunes
1oz/30g raisins
3tbsp/45ml Cointreau
Finely grated orange peel of 1 orange
4ozs/125g dessicated coconut
3ozs/85g chopped walnuts
6ozs/175g light brown sugar

Chop the apricots, prunes and raisins, put them in a bowl and pour over the liqueur. Leave bowl at room temperature for about an hour while the chopped fruits absorb the liqueur. Transfer chopped fruit to a food processor or blender to chop up finely and then mix the fruit thoroughly with 3ozs/85g of the coconut, the orange peel and the walnuts.

Mix the remaining coconut with the sugar and spread on a plate. Roll the fruit mixture into small balls and roll in the sugar mixture. Place in sweet cases and store in an airtight container.

CRYSTALLISED FRUITS

2lbs/1kg best fruit - apricots, peaches, cherries, greengages or plums
2lbs/1kg granulated sugar
8fl.ozs/250ml water

Remove skins from apricots and peaches by pouring over boiling water to split the skins. Remove stalks from cherries and extract the stones from all the fruit - using the tip of a potato peeler makes this easier.

Make a concentrated syrup by boiling together the sugar and water in a heavy based pan. Add the fruit and cook gently in the syrup until it is soft but still firm. Times will vary depending on the type of fruit. Pour fruit and syrup into bowl and leave overnight.

Return the fruit and syrup to the pan, bring to the boil and cook for 1 minute. Remove the fruit with a slotted spoon and put into a bowl. Return the syrup to the heat and cook until it becomes very thick. Pour it over the fruit and leave to stand overnight. Repeat the process once or twice more when the fruit should have absorbed all the syrup. Lay a sheet of greaseproof paper or wire rack and lay the fruit out to dry or place in a very cool oven with the doo slightly ajar until it has dried. Turn fruit occasionally while it is drying. Store in an airtight container for up to 3 months.

GLACE CHERRIES

1lb/500g stoned cherries
1lb/500g sugar
4fl.ozs/125ml water

Put the sugar and water in a heavy-based pan, bring to the boil slowly and cook until it becomes syrupy. Add the prepared cherries and simmer gently until they are soft. Leave the cherries in the syrup for 3 days and then drain them and place in a bowl. Bring the syrup to the boil and pour over the cherries and leave them for a further 3 days. Drain the cherries through a sieve and leave them to dry on a sheet of greaseproof paper on a wire rack. Store in jars lined with greaseproof paper. The syrup can be used over ice cream.

FRUIT LEATHER

lbs/1kg dried apricots
b/500g dried peaches
ing sugar

ut the dried fruit into a food processor and chop finely. Sprinkle icing sugar nickly on a board and place the fruit mixture on it. Roll the mixture out to bout 1/8"/3mm thick and cut into strips about 1"/15mm by 2"/30mm. oll each strip into a tight roll and store in an airtight tin.

PRUNE AND ALMOND FROSTING

6ozs/175g granulated sugar
2tbsp/30ml water
1tsp/5ml corn oil
Pinch of salt
1 egg white
4ozs/125g finely chopped prunes
2ozs/60g chopped almonds

Put all the ingredients, except for the prunes and almonds, in the top of a double boiler or a bowl. Beat for 1 minute with an electric or hand beater. Heat the double boiler or stand the bowl in boiling water and continue to beat until the mixture stands up in peaks. Remove from the heat and continue beating until the mixture is sufficiently thick to spread. Add the chopped prunes and almonds and mix well. Leave to set.

CHOCOLATE PRUNES

12 whole stoned prunes
12 whole Brazil nuts
8ozs/250g plain dark chocolate

Stuff the prunes with the Brazil nuts. Break up the chocolate and put in a small basin. Stand the basin in hot water over a low heat and melt the chocolate slowly. Dip the prunes into the chocolate (a cocktail stick is useful to hold the prunes), covering them completely, and place on greaseproof paper to set. Put in a covered container and store in a refrigerator.

Other fruits such as large raisins or glace cherries can also be used for this recipe.

Index

142

144